C000057835

Sisters of Secrets

The Story Of Sisters Leading Up To The Turpin Case Arrest

Elizabeth Flores

Creative Life Publishing & Learning Institute
www.CLPLI.com
Info@CLPLI.com

Book Versions
Paperback ISBN: 978-1-946265-17-3
Hardback ISBN: 978-1-946265-18-0
eBook ISBN: 978-1-946265-19-7
Amazon ISBN: 978-1-946265-20-3

Cover Design By Dara Rogers

Copyright © 2018 Elizabeth Jane Flores and CLPLI, LLC

All rights reserved. No part of this book may be reproduced in any form without prior written permission from the publisher. This work represents the views and opinions of the author alone. No liability in conjunction with the content or the use of ideas connected with this work is assumed by the publisher.

This is a work of creative nonfiction. The events are portrayed to the best of Elizabeth Flores's memory. While all the stories in this book are true, some names and identifying details have been changed to protect the privacy of the people involved. The conversations in the book all come from the author's recollections, though they are not written to represent word-for-word transcripts. Rather, the author has retold them in a way that evokes the feeling and meaning what was said and in all instances, the essence of the dialogue is accurate.

CLPLI is committed to publishing works of quality and integrity. In that spirit, we are proud to offer this book to our readers; however, the story, the experiences, and the words are the author's alone.

Mention of specific companies, organizations, or authorities in this book does not imply endorsement by the author or the publisher nor s the mention of specific companies, organizations, or authorities ply that they endorse this book, author, or the publisher.

THE HOLY BIBLE, NEW INTERNATIONAL VERSION®, NIV® Copyright © 1973, 1978, 1984, 2011 by Biblica, Inc.® Used by permission. All rights reserved worldwide.

"New International Version" and "NIV" are registered trademarks of Biblica, Inc.®.

doe
in

Dedication

I dedicate this book to my 13 nieces and nephews Jennifer, Joshua, Jessica, Jonathan, Joy, Jullianne, Jeanetta, Jordan, James, Joanna, Jolinda, Julissa, and Janna Turpin whom I love dearly.

This book was not easy to write but I knew it had to be written. When I started writing it over 2 years ago, I was writing it with the intentions of reaching women and children victims all over the world to show them they are not alone and they too can be overcomers no matter what their past is.

So when the news broke of my sister, Louise Turpin, (The Turpin Case) just a week after my book went into editing, I knew that wasn't coincidental and this book was for my precious nieces and nephews. That made all the tears, nightmares, and repressed memories while writing worth it.

I love you thirteen children more than you know! Remember these things!

1. Your past does not define your future!

2. You are not alone!

3. You are an overcomer!

4. God has you!

5. I love you all so much

Love,
Aunt Elizabeth

CONTENTS

Acknowledgment

First of all, I want to thank God for his hand of protection on me while guiding me and speaking into me. I couldn't have ever written this book without Him. I want to thank my husband, Jonathan, and our 7 children for being so supportive while I was writing this book and during this time of travel. Third, I want to thank my cousin, mentor, coach, and friend, Tricia Andreassen. She has been my ROCK. Even though this book was in editing when the news broke, I went back to add some details to the chapters to make people understand more. Adding the details was very emotional for me. So Tricia helped me through the process of adding and stayed up many nights holding me and crying with me. She has been by my side since the day news broke of my sister's arrest and has been my support in every way. I love Tricia more than she knows! Thank you to the Unstoppable Warriors for your support. Your prayers, love, and kind words have carried me through. Thank you, Edward Reed, for giving me the opportunity to speak to the students at John Hopkins University and being such a great friend and support. A special thank you to Creative Life Publishing, specifically Dara Rogers. I want to thank Dr. Oz for giving me a platform to speak out. Thank you, Dr. Oz and your whole team for such love and compassion you carry. Thank you, Mieke Brock, my best friend for years, for years of encouragement that I could accomplish this book! I love you! Last but not the least, I want to thank my Pastor, Mitchell and Janella Wright along with my church family for the support and prayers during this time and journey of my life. I am so blessed to have such wonderful people in my life!

Chapter 1
Who Would Have Known

Who Would Have Known

"Come on in here and give me a tight hug." said my Papaw.

I would come to know his silky, persuasive voice as a sign of what was to come, later in my years. But my sister knew what this dark-haired man standing tall with authority beside us wanted. She got between my 4-year-old body frame and his 6-foot physique. A man who we were told to always trust.

Turning to me, she looked at me with tears in her eyes and said, "I'll go."

I looked up to her. She was my protector; my shield. Even when Mommy and Daddy would have fights and I would shrink my body in fear, she covered my ears and pulled me into her chest to hold me tight. Yes, she was my sister and I couldn't be any prouder to call her mine. The sun rose and sat with her. She was the one that I knew I could count on, no matter what. The nurturing, loving heart that played games with me, laughed with me and took my place for the sexual abuse that happened in those dark places was a gift.

So, the night of January 15, 2018 I was rocked to my core. Could what I just heard be true? My sister? The one who had taken care of me was now the woman being seen on every International News Channel. Within hours, it was the leading story on every media outlet in the world. Louise Turpin, my sister, had just been arrested for abusing, starving, and chaining her 13 children to their beds. That was a secret that had been hidden from me, all the family and the neighbors that lived all within 20 feet of each other on their small grassy plots. That secret was being revealed and just like a big ball of yarn neatly rolled tight, the string had just become unraveled.

I felt nauseous. It had to be a nightmare, right? And I just couldn't wake up....

Within moments of hearing the news, my phone began to ring and my social media accounts were instantly bombarded. I immediately alerted my close cousin Tricia. She had become my mentor and my coach to help me through the years that had chained me in shame. I sent her the news link along with my words, "Please pray." Within minutes, she called me. Together, we began to pray for the children as this entire situation was being revealed. We tried to make sense of all this. How could this happen? I was shocked. I had no warning of the repressed memories that would come flooding back to me. A tidal wave revealing the secrets that had been ingrained in us to keep quiet; at any cost.

In those following hours that streamed into days with no end in sight, I was overwhelmed with a rollercoaster of emotions. I felt anger, sadness, confusion, hurt and thankfulness. I was angry that Louise could do something like this. I was so sad that this evil happened. I was confused at how "the sister I knew" could now have such a destructive careless heart. I was hurting so much for my nieces and nephews. I was thankful that my teenage niece had the courage to escape from their house and call for help.

The anger and confusion towards Louise and David was so strong. My mind kept whispering, Ephesians 6:12, *"For our struggle is not against flesh and blood, but against the rulers, against the authorities, against the powers of this dark world and against the spiritual forces of evil in the heavenly realms."* I held on this truth in the midst of such darkness.

All I knew to do was pray. It seemed like thousands of news reporters, shows, journalists, and the public were contacting me by phone, Facebook, Messenger, text, and even e-mail "wanting to talk to me." Within hours, my life changed dramatically.

At first, I chose to stay quiet.

God was working in my heart. I remembered the reason I had started my career in writing and speaking just two years before this. I wanted to bring hope to hurting children and women all over the world. Especially those who had experienced abuse. When I was a child, I held on to the hope of a future that would be better than the hell that I had lived in. Staring at my reflection in the mirror, I had to make a choice: stay quiet or raise my voice. Why would I remain quiet when I could make a difference?

The answer became clear. It was time. Time to let the sisterhood of secrets come out.

JULY 36, 1978
Papaw holding me.

5-7-78
Papaw is holding me in this picture. Louise is standing in front of Mamaw.

Me, Louise, Mommy, and Daddy.

Me, Papaw and Louise. Out of gathering the photos for this book this was one of the photos that has troubled me the most as I look into Louise's eyes.

House where my sister Louise and her husband David were arrested.

Me standing in the archway of my sister Louise's house where she was arrested.

Look how the houses are so close to each other.

Chapter 2
Battle Of The Heart

Battle Of The Heart

I was born in Princeton, West Virginia in the heart of the Appalachian Mountains. From the beginning, my life was filled with challenges and miracles. I came into the world with heart conditions, officially diagnosed with a heart murmur, and aortic stenosis. I had two heart valves instead of four, and if that wasn't terrible enough, one of the valves had a leak, and the other valve didn't close properly.

According to the doctors, I never should have survived. I was so weak. My fingernails and toenails were a constant purple color. I couldn't participate in gym class at school. My parents were told that I never would be able to have children because my heart was simply too weak and that having children would probably kill me. The news hurt badly. As a child playing with my dolls, I often dreamed of holding my own children one day.

When I was eight years old, my parents were asked to make a quick decision; the type that no parent would ever want to make. I needed surgery in order for me to live, but the doctor told my parents that I might not be strong enough to survive. As one might imagine, my parents experienced a wide range of emotions including fear, worry, and deep anxiety. They went straight to my grandparents, family, friends, and church. They cried and prayed. We attended the Athens Church of God the following Sunday. My Aunt Shirley, who was the pastor, picked me up and cradled me in her arms. She cried out to the Lord on my behalf. In the book of Matthew, it says, *"Again, truly I tell you that if two of you on earth agree about anything they ask for, it will be done for them by my Father in heaven. For where two or three gathers in my name, there am I with them."* (Matthew 18:19-20)

"Is anyone among you sick? Let them call the elders of the church to pray over them and anoint them with oil in the name of the Lord. And the prayer offered in faith will make the sick person well; the Lord will raise them up. If they have sinned, they will be forgiven."
James 5:14-15

The following Monday when the doctor took x-rays and performed a sonogram, my heart was whole. Do you get this? Whole! I had NO heart murmur, NO aortic stenosis, and I had four normal valves that were working correctly! The doctor was in tears. Overnight my heart murmur closed up, a leak in my valve closed up, a closing flap on another valve was gone, and a third and fourth valve had appeared. Blood was circulating perfectly, exactly the way it was supposed to be. My heart was completely normal and made whole overnight. This was a miracle! This could only be God! The doctor gave my mom and dad my earlier records with the x-rays and sonograms along with the results from that day so they could use it as a testimony. Can you imagine the difference in the atmosphere when we got that news?! My parents ran back to my grandparents, family, friends, pastor, and church. It is so important to have these people in our lives to hold us up in the bad times and rejoice with us in the good times.

"Is anyone among you in trouble? Let them pray. Is anyone happy? Let them sing songs of praise."
James 5:13

"Therefore encourage one another and build each other up, just as in fact you are doing."
1 Thessalonians 5:11

From that day forward, I was a normal child that could run, play, take gym classes, and laugh again. I love sharing this testimony. I love to tell people what God did for me at this time in my life. We are told to do this in the book of Psalms, *"Come and hear, all you who fear God; let me tell you what he has done for me."* (Psalm 66:16)

I was healed and normal. I did all the things I was told I would never do. One of my favorite things to do was playing basketball and volleyball with my boyfriend who eventually became my husband. Guess what? I could, and I did! We were young and very active. Our love grew and grew, and we were married less than a year after we started dating. The first thing we talked about was having children. I was so excited because I knew I could have children. God had healed me completely. I had 8 babies in 10 years. None of my babies were born with a heart condition although I lost number 6 (Destiny Faith) because her heart wouldn't grow with her body. When I look at myself in the mirror, I see a miracle, and I know I have a great calling. When I look at my seven beautiful children, I see a miracle. My life is a miracle.

I want you to remember this. Know that the enemy will keep trying to destroy you, bring you down, and attack you if you are a threat to him. *"The thief comes only to steal and kill and destroy; I have come that they may have life and have it to the full."* (John 10:10)

If you are a Christian, you are a threat to the enemy because everyone was put on earth for a purpose and everyone is to tell others the goodness of Christ. Your purpose may not be to preach, write books, sing, or do missions, but every one of us Christians is to tell people about Christ. The good news is that God never gives up on us and He fights for us. In Exodus 14:14 it is written, *"The Lord will fight for you, you need only to be still."*

This verse tells us that we do not have to be anguished, anxious, or discouraged when bad things happen in our lives. When a situation seems hopeless or overwhelming, we may be tempted to doubt God, but we must remember that no problem is too big for God and He will care for His children. He has promised to take care of us (Philippians 4:19), make good plans for us (Jeremiah 29:11), and to love us beyond measure (Romans 8:37-39).

We are designed to fight the enemy with the word of God and prayer. We have authority over Satan. *"I have given you the authority to trample on snakes and scorpions and to overcome all the power of the enemy; nothing will harm you."* (Luke 10:19) This verse says your authority over Satan does not rest on your strength. You cannot overcome the enemy with your power. It has to be with kingdom authority from God. As a child of God, you have His authority to overcome every attack of Satan.

Remember earlier when I shared with you about my heart condition when the enemy tried to take me out as a child? He told me I could not have children and if I tried, I would die. Then God healed me. Even though I won that battle, the enemy still pushed forward in an attack. However, with great opposition comes great blessing.

At the age of twenty-one, I had my first child, Jonathan Adam. My second child, Joseph Nathaniel, arrived when I was twenty-two years old. Everything went great. The babies were healthy and so was I. At the age of twenty-four, I had my third child, Jacob Dillon. This one didn't go so well. A sonogram taken around 3 months into the pregnancy revealed a blood clot surrounding the baby. I was told that the baby was still alive, but I would miscarry. I began praying and speaking life over him. We went back a few weeks later for another sonogram, and the doctors were shocked to discover that the blood clot was gone and Jacob Dillon was healthy and happy!

All of a sudden at six months into the pregnancy, I couldn't breathe.

At the emergency room, doctors said my oxygen level was low, and a blood clot was found in my lung. There was concern about the baby because of my oxygen level. Doctors were able to shrink the blood clot using IVs. I went into labor on the exact due date, and everything seemed to be going great until a student nurse asked if she could check me to see how far I had dilated. I said yes. She checked me, and I started pouring blood. The placenta had ripped from the uterus. The baby's heart rate was dropping, and he wasn't getting enough oxygen. I was losing way too much blood too fast. I passed out. They told my husband Jonathan that both of our lives were at risk. Plans were made to rush me in for a C-section, but the baby's head was already too far down. At this point, the doctor took me from six to ten centimeters with his hand and suctioned the baby out. The baby was rushed to the NICU while they continued to work on me. We left the hospital in just a few days, and we are both healthy and normal today.

At the age of twenty-six, I had my fourth child, Nicole Elizabeth. Everything went great. She was healthy. At the age of twenty-eight, my fifth child, Elisha Gabriel, was born. This pregnancy was not so easy. It started off great. Throughout the nine months, I was carrying a healthy baby as far as we could tell. Labor was normal and uneventful. However, by the next day, it was obvious that something was wrong He couldn't keep any of the milk down and was losing weight quickly. The doctors said he had a failure to thrive and ordered tests to determine why. Elisha Gabriel's esophagus wasn't fully developed. He was in the hospital for a long time before we took him home. Afterward, he was diagnosed with Respiratory Syncytial Virus (RSV), which can be very serious for infants and older adults. Several times his oxygen level dropped. Because he was in the hospital so much, Elisha Gabriel was very delayed with crawling, sitting, walking, and talking. The doctors told us the part of the brain that controls speech was damaged and warned that the lack of oxygen could affect his mental capacity.

My husband and I refused to believe this. We prayed and were very careful what we spoke over him because words are powerful. With our word and actions, we reinforced the faith that everything was normal. We never repeated what the doctor said. The family didn't even know. Let me just say at the time of this writing Elisha Gabriel is a healthy, normal, and thriving teen boy that talks great and plays on his school football and wrestling teams!

At the age of twenty-nine, I had my sixth child, Destiny Faith. This is the most difficult thing I've ever gone through. About 16 weeks into the pregnancy, my sonogram revealed a problem. Destiny Faith's heart was not growing, and I was told I would miscarry her. A few weeks later, I started bleeding and went to the hospital. My water broke, and she was born. Destiny Faith did not make it. At that time, I had to choose my actions. I was emotionally wrecked in every way, but I accepted that she was with Jesus. I allowed the Lord to carry me. It would have been easy for me to be angry with God and turn my back on Him, but I knew I needed Him.

At the age of thirty, my seventh child, Ariel Gabrielle arrived in the world. Everything went well, and thankfully, she was healthy. At the age of thirty-one, I had my eighth child, William (Will) James. The enemy really hit hard with this one. My husband and I separated while I was pregnant (I'll get into that in another chapter of this book) and I was very depressed. The doctors offered to prescribe medicine for depression, but explained it would be harmful to the baby. I refused to take the medicine because I was worried about the baby. When I gave birth, there were complications. William spent a couple of weeks in the NICU. He was purple. He was placed on oxygen and a feeding tube. I couldn't even nurse him. Again, I grabbed hold of God, and He pulled me through with prayers.

The enemy first tried to take my life physically. He continued in my childhood through the sexual abuse, the living environment I was staying in as a child, and then again as an adult by trying to take out some of my children. He didn't stop there. There are many chapters in my life where the enemy continued to attempt to destroy me, but it only made me stronger and stronger.

Let your heart be encouraged by these scriptures:

"And the God of all grace, who called you to his eternal glory in Christ, after you have suffered a little while, will himself restore you and make you strong, firm and steadfast."
1 Peter 5:10

"Be joyful in hope, patient in affliction, faithful in prayer."
Romans 12:12

"No temptation has overtaken you except what is common to mankind. And God is faithful; he will not let you be tempted beyond what you can bear. But when you are tempted, he will also provide a way out so that you can endure it." (1 Corinthians 10:13) The word temptation doesn't only mean being tempted to sin. In the Greek language, it also means a time of trial or time of testing.

God tells us that there is no trial that we may go through that is not common to man. There are times when we feel that no one can understand what we are going through. The truth is, others have gone through very similar trials. God helped them through it, and He will do the same for you. You will be given grace by God to get through the trials. Second, God tells us in this verse that He will not allow us to be tested beyond what we are able to endure. God knows us better than anyone, even better than we know ourselves. He knows exactly how much we can take. He promises that He will never allow you to be tested more than you can bear. Third, He promises that with the temptation, He will make a way to escape so you can bear it. When we can see no hope whatsoever of getting out, He says, I will make a way to escape. At just the right time and in just the right way, He will open the door.

In the Bible, it is written, *"I have told you these things, so that in me you may have peace. In this world, you will have trouble. But take heart! I have overcome the world."* (John 16:33)

Jesus was clear that this isn't a perfect world, but we have hope because Jesus has overcome the world. There is nothing that you are facing that Jesus Christ has not overcome. Don't let your circumstances have the final word.

Although I had struggles of my physical heart (and the healing that took place), you will see the brokenness of what was in my spirit and the secrets I had to carry down in my heart.

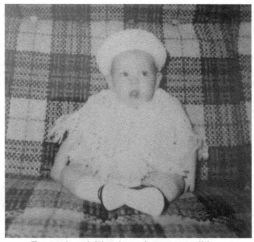

From day 1 I had my heart condition.

My family has been such a blessing from God.

Chapter 3
Feeling Alone

Feeling Alone

"No one likes me," I sat crying on the bed talking to Louise. "What are they doing to you?" she asked.

"They're teasing me, and they are calling me names! They won't even play with me, Louise!"

Being in the second grade, I wanted to have friends. When I told my big sister my troubles, she wrapped her arms around me. She even went next door to our childhood neighbor Vicky and asked her to defend me at school. Thank goodness I had my sis. She was my best friend.

By the third grade, I grew more insecure and withdrawn. Other kids quit talking to me and now my big sister had left me all alone. She had run away to Texas to get married. I didn't know what to do. The rough times continued in the fourth and fifth grade. I had no friends at all. Time at school was difficult and uncomfortable. My grades dropped. It was a hard time hearing and remembering anything the teacher taught. It got so bad I refused to do my homework so that my name would be written on the blackboard and I would not be allowed to go to recess. I didn't want to be alone at recess. I felt ugly, insecure, scared, embarrassed, and sad.

Home life wasn't much better. I found negativity everywhere I turned. My parents got divorced. Mommy was in and out of abusive relationships and other awful things. My Papaw was molesting me. I was physically, mentally, and emotionally abused by two other people as well. I held my head low and rarely made eye contact with anyone. I felt all alone, notice I said I "felt!" I come to tell you today that you are never alone! God is always there by your side. The book of Deuteronomy tells us, *"The Lord is the one who goes ahead of you; He will be with you he will not fail you or forsake you. Do not fear or be dismayed."* Not only does God not leave us alone, but he goes ahead of us... before us! I became so insecure that if someone spoke to me, my face turned blood red and I became teary-eyed.

The problems I experienced stemmed from my home life. It was so messed up. I felt so unworthy and unsure. As a result, I had low self-esteem. Kids could sense that and fed off of it. It wasn't everyone, but I felt as if though it was everyone. In the seventh grade, I met a friend, Jennifer. Her friends became my friends, and things improved significantly at school. By the time I enrolled in middle school, God had completed a lot of work in my heart. The faith in my little girl heart blossomed because I believed He would be there for me even if no one else would be. I did a daily exercise where I looked at myself in the mirror and said, "I am beautiful." After a while, I felt and believed that I was beautiful. My self-esteem lifted and things changed at school. Keep in mind, I was still being sexually, physically, mentally, and emotionally abused. However, God was teaching me to fight. Physical abuse made me feel weak. The mental abuse made me feel stupid, ugly, and anything but good. Emotional abuse made me feel like I had no value as a person.

These are the prayers and passages that got me through:

- **Pray.** Ask God for help and experience victory with His power. The book of Timothy tells us *"Therefore I want the men everywhere to pray, lifting up holy hands without anger or disputing."* (1 Timothy 2:8)

In the book of John, we learn, *"And we know that he hears us –*

whatever we ask– we know that we have what we asked of him." (1 John 5:15)

- **Speak and believe the truth.** There is power in faith and your tongue! In the book of James and Proverbs, we see confirmation of this. *"But when you ask, you must believe and not doubt, because the one who doubts is like a wave of the sea, blown and tossed by the wind."* (James 1:6)

  "The tongue has the power of life and death, and those who love it will eat its fruit." (Proverbs 18:21)

  "The words of the reckless pierce like swords, but the tongue of the wise brings healing." (Proverbs 12:18)

- **Choose not to be afraid.** When we panic, it's hard to speak positive and truth. Pray! *"Say to those with fearful hearts, be strong, do not fear; your God will come, he will come with vengeance; with divine retribution, he will come to save you."* (Isaiah 35:4)

- **Give it to God. Let go!** Lay it at His feet and walk away! We are directed to do this in the book of Psalms, *"Cast your burden on the Lord, and he shall sustain you; he shall never permit the righteous to be moved."* (Psalm 55:22)

- **Surrender and watch God work.** *"Come and see the works of God; He is awesome in his doing toward the sons of men."* (Psalm 66:5)

By middle school, God had transformed me to where I was treated differently. My self-esteem had changed, and so did my surroundings in the school environment. I still had the problems at home, but I found better ways to cope with them.

Every day when I looked in the mirror, I preached to myself, "I am beautiful. I am a child of God. I am fearfully and wonderfully made. I am loved. I am the head and not the tail. I am above and not beneath."

I had to cling to God and speak positive life into everything. *"I will praise you, for I am fearfully and wonderfully made, Marvelous are your works, and that my soul knows very well."* (Psalm 139:14) God had his hand on me; to be so young and know how to do this was something that most kids didn't know to do.

I had friends and came out of my shell. Those who know me now could never imagine me being shy and especially quiet. That's funny! It's true I was at one time shy and quiet. By my second semester of college, I had come completely out of my shell. Wow, there was a big difference. Now I can't shut up! Haha! God had to break me out of my shell to use me in my calling. Now, look at me! I was not qualified, but I was called. God worked in me, and here I am. God doesn't call the qualified, He qualifies the called!

I want you to be encouraged right now. Let no one define who you are through abuse, words or deeds!

> *"For you see your calling, brethren, that not many wise according to the flesh, not many mighty, not many noble, are called. But God has chosen the foolish things of the world to put to shame the wise, and God has chosen the weak things of the world to put to shame the things which are mighty; and the base things of the world and the things which are despised God has chosen, and the things which are not, to bring nothing the things that are, that no flesh should glory in his presence."*
> 1 Corinthians 1:26-29

I held on and kept depending on God for strength and waited

for positive change to grow in my life. Sometimes faith is just continuing to walk when we don't feel like it until situations change. Resilience emerges when we lean on Him and continue to bounce back even after the entire world seems to be against you.

Louise was my best friend and big sister.

Chapter 4
My Sister Leaving Home

My Sister Leaving Home

My mom and dad had three girls. I was the middle child. My oldest sister Louise was always protective of me. She was eight years older and my best friend. We loved playing cards, jacks, and board games together. We would play house like she was my mom. I still remember how much she loved The Chipmunks and how she would listen to them on a record player. We would record ourselves together, and she would leave me messages on the tape player. I always thought she was the best big sister ever!

About age 15, Louise dated a guy from our church and in just a short time they got serious. They seemed to always be talking. She was crazy about him, and he seemed to like her.

I remember the night she secretly pulled me into her bedroom to talk. "Hey Elizabeth," she whispered. "Come in here I want to talk to you." I came in excited because I felt she would tell me a secret because of the tone of her voice.

"What would you think if I got married?" she questioned. I loved that she was asking me! My 8-year-old self didn't know what to say, but she went on. "You know… if I get married, I'll have a really nice house, and you'll get to come visit all the time and hang out with me. You can stay overnight too."

That got me even more excited, but what really got me going was, "And when I have a baby someday, you can come and play with the baby and hold it." My mind raced, and I thought how cool it would be that she would have all this and still be living close by. I would get to see her all the time and play house!

That is when she got a duffle bag and threw stuff in. "Now I trust you," she said, "don't tell anybody that we talked about this." Of course, I promised I wouldn't but what I didn't understand is what would happen next.

The next morning, we woke up and went to school like any normal day. After school was over, I went home, but Louise did not. Mommy thought maybe she missed the bus, so she drove up to the school to find out where she was. The school told Mommy that Daddy had checked her out. That prompted her to call Daddy right away, and he flipped out! That's when things got bad. I heard them talking, and Daddy did not check her out. The school explained that a tall man wearing a hat and had facial hair (which we discovered was fake) had come in and claimed to be her dad. He had checked her out of school.

My parents were frantic and went to the police. I think it was three days later they found her with her boyfriend, David in Fort Worth, Texas (which was about a seventeen-hour drive from where we lived). David was six and a half years older than her, so that legally constituted kidnapping. He was almost 23, and she was just 16. But, because we all went to church together for years and his parents were friends with my parents, they decided not to press charges. My parents made him bring her back and after discussion, they told her she could get married. They had a small church wedding and headed back to Fort Worth, Texas. I remember the whole time she was gone, I was so worried. I cried and cried.

When she got married, and I realized she was moving so far away, I was scared, sad, and angry. I felt betrayed. I was scared because she was always there for me. She had protected me a lot. When Mommy and Daddy would fight, she would hide my face in her chest and hold my ears. She would take my place when my Papaw who sexually abused me would come after me. My heart was broken that she wouldn't be close anymore. At just eight years old, my whole world felt like it was falling apart. I felt betrayed because she made it sound like she would live close and I could spend nights with her. She had painted this picture, and I can still see it today like I could that night she talked in her bedroom.

Life was so different without her. My parents started not to get along even more. I felt sad all the time. It was just me and my baby sister Teresa who was just three years old. I didn't have an older sister to look up to anymore. Louise would send me letters. I would get so excited to get a mail with my name on it. I loved reading what she had to say. I loved getting phone calls from her, but I still missed her so much. That summer, we got to ride on an airplane to visit her. Four years later, she had her first baby, Jennifer. By this time, they had moved from Texas to California. We went to visit them and took an Amtrak train from West Virginia. It was during Christmas break of my sixth-grade year, and we visited for 3 weeks. She took us to Disneyland, Universal Studios, Movie Land, and some other awesome places. This was a trip I would never forget. Everything seemed to be just like she had said. I was getting to visit and spend the night and hold her baby but very different from the way an eight-year-old's little mind had pictured it. When I was little, I had thought I would see her every day and spend weekends with her, not see her just once a year. In reality, I understood the truth of it all. My sister loved me and now looking back I think the reason she talked to me in her room was because she wanted my approval. I believe that is also why she made it sound the way she did.

Where Louise had become my comforter, my protector, and my friend, it was now God who became my comforter, my protector, and my friend. To this day, I am reminded of these scriptures. Over time, I came to know God had to be my real protector in life.

*"Praise be to the God and Father of our Lord Jesus Christ,
the Father of compassion and the God of all comfort, who
comforts us in all our troubles, so that we can comfort those in any
trouble with the comfort we ourselves receive from God."*
2 Corinthians 1:3-4

*"Whoever dwells in the shelter of the Most High will rest in
the shadow of the Almighty. I will say of the Lord, "He is my
refuge and my fortress, my God, in whom I trust. Surely, he will
save you from the fowler's snare and from the deadly pestilence.
He will cover you with his feathers, and under his wings you will
find refuge; his faithfulness will be your shield and rampart."*
Psalm 91:1-4

*"Greater love has no one than this: to lay down one's
life for one's friends."*
John 15:13

Life changes aren't easy. They can bring us down. They can make us have all kinds of feelings such as anxiety, sadness, fear, excitement, and much more. The way we feel often depends on the situation and the change that comes with it. Sometimes it feels like, as soon as we get back up from a punch, something else hits. I didn't realize that I was building my strength in those moments as a child. I knew God was my source. I decided I was going to just give it to God and go on with life.

I had Mommy and Daddy, but they fought all the time. My parents separated and divorced just months after my sister left home and I still believe her leaving contributed to that situation. They argued over my dad signing for her to get married—A LOT.

No matter what life throws at you, get up and fight!

I want you to be encouraged not to let situations get in your way because what the enemy means for bad, God can turn around for good! It might not happen instantly, but He won't let you down.

My Great-Grandpa, Poppy, had a favorite scripture and it has been one I have come to rely on. My cousin Tricia told me one day that on the day he died, he was quoting it from memory. *"And we know that in all things God works for the good of those who love him, who have been called according to his purpose."* (Romans 8:28)

That is what I held onto in the middle of my parents' divorce and the crumbling.

Louise at 6 years old.

Louise at 10 years old.

Louise on her 10th birthday!

LOUISE   OCT. 17, 1982

Two years before Louise left home.

LOUISE "DADDY'S GIRL"
COMING FROM SCHOOL
3:50PM FRIDAY MAR. 25, 1983

Right before Louise left home.

LOUISE   LOUISE

12-25-84

Louise's last Christmas living
at home sitting beside maternal
grandmother (Mamaw) "Louise"
who Louise was named after.

David and Louise pictured right after
Louise's high school graduation.

David and Louise's wedding picture.

David and Louise early years of
marriage.

David and Louise Christmas in early
years of marriage.

Christmas at Daddy's few years after marriage.

Chapter 5
My Parent's Divorce

My Parent's Divorce

The screaming and yelling were the worst I had ever heard.

Shrinking down in the other room with little Teresa hugging me tight I heard, "Who are you talking to?" Daddy said to Mommy.

She lied and didn't tell him the truth. I think she told him she was talking to Papaw. But he already knew it wasn't true. Just moments before, I had gone into their bedroom where Daddy was already asleep for the night because he had to get up early for work the next day. I overheard Mommy having this phone conversation that didn't seem right. Feeling something "off," I had gone into the bedroom and said, "Daddy, I think Mommy is on the phone with somebody. I think something is funny." He picked up the receiver and listened to the conversation. I knew Mommy was seeing someone else and I couldn't take it anymore. I was hurt that Daddy worked so hard all the time and Mommy didn't have to work. He was good to us, and I couldn't understand how Mommy could treat him so bad and be so mean by being with somebody else.

The argument got so bad, I was shaking. I ran out of the house, in the dark to get away from it. While I was outside, I saw Papaw in the driveway.

Papaw told Daddy, "You better get out of here because if you don't, I'm calling the police."

"I want a few minutes with my daughters."

Daddy sat us down on the couch and broke the news. Kneeling down in front of us, he put one hand on each of our knees. He explained to Teresa and me, "Daddy has to go away for a little while. Mommy and Daddy need a break. I am going to move into another house close by. You can come and see me any time you want. I'll make sure that the judge gives me rights to see you."

But at eight and three years old, we didn't understand what all that meant. We were crying our eyes out. I was frozen sitting there with my hands in my lap. I didn't even look at Teresa; I knew if I did I would shatter. He got up off his knees and walked out of the door.

The only two adults left in the house were Mommy and Papaw. My Papaw that touched me and made me feel so dirty and bad all the time. That brought another level of anxiety. Nothing was safe anymore. Louise had left, and now Daddy was leaving. After he left, Mommy got mad at us, and we got in trouble for crying over Daddy leaving.

Standing by our living room lamp and looking out through the window the next day, reality hit me. I had such a sadness because I knew Daddy was gone. All I could do was cry. As the days followed, Daddy would come by after work. But Mommy wouldn't let him in the house. We had to go out to the driveway and visit with him. He would ask if he could take us for ice cream or do something special. Most times she said, "No." But the times when she let us go with him, we were so happy. I could hardly stand being away from him.

Now more than ever I was scared, torn, and heartbroken. I thought something was wrong with me and didn't know how to fix "me." Life became weird. It felt so different. I was having a hard time getting used to not having both parents at home. Finally, I could go to visit my dad. It was a funny feeling going to stay with him on the weekends instead of having him home all the time. My emotions were all over the place. I blamed myself for what happened.

I kept thinking, "I should have said nothing to Daddy, and we would all still be together." I was such a Daddy's girl and attached to his hip. That thought was eating me up inside. I wanted to go back and have a "do over." I had no one to talk to because I didn't want it to get back to Mommy that it was my fault he left. I told Daddy to pick up the phone on the other receiver that night. That was a secret he took to his grave.

I used to think that Mommy should hate me, distrust me, and never want to speak to me again. So, even into my adult life, I thought that's what would happen if she found out. We always had relationship problems. I always felt like I didn't belong. I always felt like Mommy treated me differently from the other kids and I didn't want to make it worse.

I loved Mommy and Daddy so much. I tried holding my emotions in or keep control of them without showing my anger and hurt because I didn't want to make them feel worse. My 8-year-old mind thought I needed to hold it all together. Since I was raised up in church, I knew to turn to God. So that's what I did. I prayed.

Psalm 55:22 says, *"Cast your cares on the Lord and he will sustain you; he will never let the righteous be shaken."*

1 Peter 5:7 says, *"Cast all your anxiety on him because he cares for you."*

I cried out to God, and I felt his arms around me.

Philippians 4:6,7 says, *"And the peace of God, which transcends all understanding, will guard your hearts and your minds in Christ Jesus."*

I began to believe that everything would be alright.

Psalm 16:8 says, *"I keep my eyes always on the Lord. With him at my right hand, I will not be shaken."*

The fear faded.

Isaiah 41:10 says, *"So do not fear, for I am with you; do not be dismayed, for I am your God. I will strengthen you and help you; I will uphold you with my righteous right hand."*

Faith rose in me and helped me to move on. Life kept going, and I could make the new "normal."

Jeremiah 17:7-8 told me, *"But blessed is the one who trusts in the Lord, whose confidence is in him. They will be like a tree planted by the water that sends out its roots by the stream. It does not fear when heat comes; its leaves are always green. It has no worries in a year of drought and never fails to bear fruit."*

Proverbs 3:5-6 encouraged me to, *"Trust in the Lord with all your heart and lean not on your own understanding; in all your ways submit to him, and he will make your paths straight."*

Psalm 56:3 comforted me with, *"When I am afraid, I put my trust in you."*

With God by my side, he helped me through all of it. That doesn't mean it didn't hurt. It means I could hold to His strength and not give up. I bounced back. Just remember that life circumstances don't have to be the draining weight that takes you down. You can fight it. With determination, faith, and God's Word, He will always be by your side.

Deuteronomy 31:8 reminded me, *"The Lord himself goes before you and will be with you; he will never leave you nor forsake you. Do not be afraid; do not be discouraged."*

With God all things are possible.

In Matthew 19:26, Jesus looked at them and said, *"With man this is impossible, but with God all things are possible."*

I pray that throughout this book, you become encouraged, have a stronger faith, learn to turn to God's Word, and fight like never before. He loves all his children the same! If He has been on my side fighting for me my whole life, then he will do the same for you throughout your life. Be encouraged as I continue to share with you about a very hard time in my life.

Me and Teresa. Easter with Daddy.

ELIZABETH
TERESA
12-25-84

Me and Teresa. Last christmas before Daddy left.

ELIZABETH
TERESA

12-25-8

Me and Teresa. Last christmas before
Daddy left.

The house Daddy bought and moved
into about 5 minutes from us after the
divorce.

Me and Teresa at Daddy's on
weekend visit.

Daddy made me a birthday cake for
my 17th birthday. Me and Teresa.

Daddy when he and Mommy fell in love.

Mommy when she first met Daddy.

When we were all a family.

Chapter 6
Sisterhood Of Dirty Secrets

Sisterhood Of Dirty Secrets

The earliest memory I have is at about four years old. I remember being told by Papaw, "You better keep this quiet. If you tell your Daddy, you know how mad he'll get, and he might hurt me. You know if he does that, he will go to jail."

My heart raced as I listened to him. I didn't want my Daddy in jail! I couldn't wrap my little mind around what Papaw was doing and why he would say such things. I was told to keep a secret, and it could not leave the family.

I knew if I told anyone there would be consequences. He also threatened, "You know if you tell anyone, someone will come and take you away from Mommy and you will never see her again." That terrified me! I could be taken away from Mommy and Teresa and also my Daddy; so I stayed quiet. I also thought if what Papaw was doing was so bad, he would go to jail and then my family would hate me. I felt so ashamed of what was being done to me; I couldn't even speak it if I wanted to.

It got much worse, like a nightmare. One day Mommy said she would take us over to Papaw's because he would give her some money. She put little Teresa and me in the car, and we headed over just a few minutes away.

When we got there, Papaw greeted us with his same sweet voice he always had and said, "Come on girls, let me show you my basement I am building." He led little Teresa and me down the stairs. There was one big room that had dirt for walls, and there was no light. It was scary down there and kinda felt like a grave or something.

There was one chair. He sat down on the chair and put me up on his lap. Poor little Teresa was forced to watch. She was about 4 years old because by this time I was about 9. I can remember her crying in the dark room while Papaw did stuff to me because she had no choice but to watch. She knew what was coming next. Once he was done with me, he would remind me again of all the reasons not to tell, and then he would pick up little Teresa and do the same thing.

The first time it happened, I let out a scream and tried to run from him, but he grabbed my arm from behind. He put his hand over my mouth to shush me. I knew Mommy was letting it happen because we were told that we had to go.

When we got there, she said, "Now ya'll girls go play with Papaw a while." Sometimes we had to go over there more than once a week and every single time the same thing happened. She got her money from Papaw, and we went back home. I'm sure Mommy thought I was too young to realize what she was doing, but I wasn't. Sometimes I think she may have just thought I was just stupid or thought they were sneaky enough about it because this continued through my teenage years. I always prayed for it to stop. I didn't want to go around my Papaw. I had no choice.

To this day, even after years of therapy, I have to sleep with some light on. When we travel, Tricia, my cousin, helps me a lot. I don't know how many times I have called her my rock. At home, my sweet husband Johnathon gives me feelings of safety. Since the news broke about Louise, I have had nightmares. Tricia has cried in my arms reliving her childhood abuse from Papaw and other men. But we know we have to stay united because we hope that we can help others reveal the dark secrets that hold them captive.

When I was about 10 years old, Mamaw and I were sitting on her swing, and we talked about things. I loved Mamaw so much and she was so good to me. We did things together all the time like go to Chick-fil-A every Saturday. To this day, it's still my favorite place to go because it's one of my all-time favorite memories. She gave me security.

While we sat there swinging, Mamaw said, "Has your Papaw ever hurt you?" I was quiet for a minute and then she continued, "If he has I'll kill him!" When Mamaw said that I said, "No." I took it literal that Mamaw would kill him. I didn't want Mamaw to go to jail for doing that. Papaw had already warned me that Daddy would get in trouble if I told. "Are you sure? You'd tell me right?" I nodded but couldn't look at her because I was ashamed for telling Mamaw that lie. "Your Papaw is not a good man. I know he has been bad to some other girls," she said. She told me that one day she had walked in on Papaw raping Louise. That is why she ended up divorcing him shortly after that.

It wasn't until many years later as an adult, I came to find out that he molested other cousins in the family. One night, Tricia (we called her Patty growing up) who lived in North Carolina, and I had a long conversation on the phone. She was going through her own memories of childhood abuse and asked me if Uncle John (my Papaw) had touched me. I told her yes, but nothing to the detail that I am now sharing. When Mamaw died in 2013, Tricia drove from North Carolina to West Virginia for the funeral. Within minutes of being in the funeral home, she suddenly said she needed to get back home, using snow as an excuse. She didn't explain until much later as we collaborated on this book and shared our dark secrets. When Papaw showed up at the funeral, she was overcome with such anxiety and anger; she left within minutes of him showing up in the room where Mamaw was laid out. I did not understand how much she had been affected until that moment. That opened the door for us to talk more. None of us girls, sisters or cousins had talked about it. Tricia told me she had told her parents and my Mamaw. But the only advice they had given her was, "Just stay away from him." Tricia later confided in me that her sister's husband had french kissed her in the basement of her sister's home one summer when she was just 9 years old.

We now realize there is a sisterhood of secrets that ties many of us in this world together. Yes, we are Sisters Of Secrets.

I often get asked how I could care for my Papaw. To be a Christian means to be Christ-like. No sin of any kind could make God not love someone. Hate is a sin. No one is worth going to hell over, so I choose not to be bitter toward him. Since I've grown up, I have had little contact and have avoided him. There is no way I would ever allow my children to be alone with this man. One time it could not be avoided. I remember the day when my Mamaw (Mommy's mom) passed away. The whole family went to the gathering at his house, but my children were to stay right with me, and I couldn't stand to stay long. It brought back too many memories, and I didn't even want my kids to be in the same room with him.

All I know is God helped me to forgive. God protected me from the hatred and bitterness that could affect my relationship with Him. I've only been to visit about three times in the 20 years of my marriage. Just because I choose to forgive and love this person doesn't mean I have to be around him and act like he did nothing.

Because of God in my life, I knew I had to pray for him and me. I always prayed he would get saved and that God would protect me from holding a grudge or unforgiveness for this person. God did just that. God helped me to understand that, *"We wrestle not against flesh and blood, but against principalities, powers, against the rulers of the darkness of this world, against spiritual wickedness in the high places."* (Ephesians 6:12)

With faith, I prayed that one day everything would be better and for forgiveness. My relationship with God, at such a young age, made the difference not to let hatred form in my heart like cancer. I knew only He could give the forgiveness to the level needed.

Few people knew this about me until I became a writer. I fought the anger. I see this man still living in his 90s, yet I lost my mom suddenly at sixty-six years old and three months later, lost my Daddy to a long illness at sixty-seven years old. I would ask myself, "Why is this person who did this awful stuff to me, my sisters, and my cousins still living?" I cried out to God why he would take my mom so suddenly, so young and he would allow someone like him still walk the earth at such an old age. Then I remember that I prayed for his salvation and God still needs to work on him.

There may be people in life you need to forgive. I want you to know that God will help take the bitterness and hatred out of your heart. Just know that God can and will. Perhaps you need to pray for someone who has hurt you. Start by praying for forgiveness and asking Him to remove the hatred and lack of forgiveness in your heart. Pray that He would help you forgive and see the person through the eyes of Jesus. Pray for that person and salvation. God will start the process. It will make you feel a lot better too. Holding on to unforgiveness hurts you more than the person you have chosen not to forgive.

Me in kindergarten.

Me in 1st grade.

Me at 7 years old.

Me and Teresa.

Me and Teresa.

My husband Jonathan, Me, and Mamaw.

Me and Teresa.

Me and Teresa.

Mamaw and Papaw before they
divorced.

Chapter 7
Life With A Troubled Mother

Life With A Troubled Mother

When I was ten years old, Mommy dated a guy named Bill. He was a great guy, and they got serious fast. He was good to us kids, and I liked him. She was so happy. My dad had a lot of respect for him because he was good to us. Soon he asked her to marry him. I remember being so happy for us. Then we found out she was expecting a baby. He bought a new house for us. I remember seeing that house for the first time when it didn't even have furniture. I remember thinking everything would be good. Our family turmoil was ending, and we would have a normal life again.

He said, "Come on little one, let's do something special for our birthday!" He was smiling so big. I loved sharing my birthday with Bill. I knew everyone would have such a good time. He took us to an amusement park, and we rode all the rides together. Teresa and I loved him so much to the point we missed him when he wasn't around. He had become part of our life; our family. It was just a couple of weeks prior to what happened….

Bill had this interesting thing about him. He didn't believe in saying the word, "Bye." He always said 'bye' meant forever. He would always say, "See you later!" One night, I remember my sister and I crying because we didn't want him to leave for his job. As he left the driveway and went down the hill, he hollered, "Bye!" That bothered my mom all night.

The following morning, he never came home from work. My mom called but couldn't get a hold of him. She knew that wasn't like him and she was worried sick. Two days later, we were at Mamaw's. Mommy was reading the paper, and she saw the obituary with his name. She screamed and about fell over. We were all devastated. We were told he had a brain tumor, and it busted on the way home from work. The car went over the mountain right across from the kitchen window of the new house. He was found by the neighbor at the bottom of the mountain. He broke his neck and died. Again, there was heartache in my little girl heart.

A few months later, Mommy had a handsome baby boy that looked just like Bill, and she named him after Bill as a Jr. She had three girls already. Bill had four girls from his previous marriage. They both wanted a boy so bad, and they got one. However, Bill never got to find out he was a boy.

After Bill died, Mommy couldn't handle the sadness, and she was drowning financially. She slept with guys for money. She put herself in dangerous places. She left us at home by ourselves a lot of times and all night. Louise was married, and so far away. I was eleven, my little sister was six, and Billy was just a little bitty baby. I was terrified of the dark. I would lock us all up in the bathroom, and we would stay up all night. Sometimes she would take us with her.

I was always so tired in school. My grades were suffering. I didn't know if Mommy would come home safe. I cried myself to sleep many times. She was once a good Christian woman. She knew right from wrong. I always longed for the day she would turn back to God. She would get with some mean and scary men. She would say, "But it makes money." That was how she looked at it. I remember one particular customer that Mommy would pick up from the bar, after he had been drinking, in downtown Princeton on Mercer Street. This man used to scare me so bad. One night when Mommy went to pick him up, he was talking about robbing a church. The next time Mommy got a phone call in the middle of the night to go pick him up from the bar, she loaded us up and went to get him. I remember being scared to death. I prayed. We were sitting in front of the bar waiting. I was sitting in the back seat and praying, "Please Lord let him not come out, and I will serve you for the rest of my life." Mommy was getting mad. He was taking so long she even sent someone in after him. He never came out, so we left. That night I knew God answered my prayers. I took it a step further and asked God never to let mom hear from him or see him ever again. Do you know that was the last time she ever heard from him? She never saw him or had contact with him ever again.

Even though I was just a little girl, I always worried about Mommy like I was her mother. I remember always trying to go with her because I felt I needed to protect her. "When I take you with me, he's nicer," she explained. "They behave, and I sure could use you. Please don't go over to your father's this weekend," she begged. "The beatings are worse when you don't go." That made me need to protect my mom. She should have been watching out for me and protecting me, but she didn't.

I always felt like Mommy didn't feel that she deserved better. She was abused all her life. She always got into situations where she needed money again and she ran to men to get it. She had several men at once. They would give her money, and she will give them sex. To her, that was like having multiple boyfriends. But to me, after seeing her all those years prostituting and taking money to let Papaw do what he did to us, I knew it was just prostitution. She made it look like they were just boyfriends.

However, I loved Mommy, and I never stopped praying for her. What I want you to see is that God was so faithful to my prayers. God kept pulling us out of awful situations. We have our own free will. He will never force you to do right. You make your own choices, then there are consequences. People who pray know what He can do. I was a little girl who was worried, scared, and sad. I cried out to the Lord, and He was faithful every time. Sometimes right away and sometimes years later. I come to tell you today that God is faithful. Keep praying! Keep believing! Keep holding on! No matter how long it takes, keep believing!

2 Thessalonians 3:3 says, *"But the Lord is faithful, and he will strengthen you and protect you from the evil one."*

Psalm 91:4 says, *"He will cover you with his feathers, and under his wings you will find refuge; his faithfulness will be your shield and rampart."*

Even when I had nightmares, God showed me over and over his protection and faithfulness. When I look back over my life, there were so many times that I was in dangerous situations. God protected me every time. Faith helped me to stand strong and be resilient in the troubles I faced.

Let me say, God is good, and I kept my promise of serving God the rest of my life that I prayed that night in the car. I'm in my forties, and I am still serving God.

Even when she got herself into another relationship that took us even on a deeper path of uncertainty, I thank God for Him never leaving me. Now, I will share with you the next man Mommy got involved with.

ELIZABETH,
& PHYLLIS
4-29-83

Me and Mommy.

Louise, Mommy holding Teresa, and me.

Mommy, Teresa, and me.

Chapter 8
Please Don't Hurt Mommy

Please Don't Hurt Mommy

"I have to meet somebody behind the post office. So, you just sit in the car and wait on me." Mommy didn't want us to know who she was meeting. He drove up at the same time as we did, so I saw who he was.

He worked as a bus driver and a janitor at our school. I recognized him right away when he walked up to the window. He said, "You know me." That day they talked for quite a while.

After that day, they dated, but it wasn't normal dating. He cleaned the school at night. Mommy would put us in the car, and we would go over to the school. We would keep him company while he cleaned. He told us that his wife had died, and he was a widower. He seemed okay at first, but there was something about him that made me feel uncomfortable.

It was like a whirlwind romance. In a short time, it seemed like they were practically living together, floating between their two houses. She would go over to his house, and he would come over to ours. Even though I was young, I could see a change began to happen. A few months into the relationship, she became obsessed with him.

One time after school, Mommy saw him talking with another school teacher. She screamed at him, "Are you seeing her?"

He yelled back, "Woman, you are crazy!"

She wanted to know where he was at all times. She would check to make sure he wasn't lying. She started accusing him of cheating. When he would watch television, she would accuse him of looking at women on TV. He lost it. He started screaming at her a lot which led to shoving. The shoving led to hitting. Eventually, Mommy was taking beatings constantly. She was a human punching bag; getting beat on about three to four times a day. I lived in constant fear.

It's hard for a child to watch this, especially to their mom. I was confused because she kept going back for more. I knew she didn't enjoy it. I couldn't figure out why she would want to be with him.

I would ask her, "Mommy, why do you stay with him?"

"Because, baby, I love him." But when they would fight, she would say, "I hate his guts!" That confused me even more.

I thought, "Is this what *love* is?" I just couldn't wrap my brain around such things.

One day, she got it into her mind that he had another woman over at his house. "You've got a woman over there, don't you? You are hiding it! I'm comin' over!" When she got off the phone, she said, "I know he's got someone over there."

She loaded us up in the car, and we went over to his house. When we showed up, he got so mad. You could see pure evil on his face. We watched and screamed as he beat her. This time was so bad, she drove herself bleeding all over the place, to the emergency room. They admitted her, and she was there about a week. The police asked if she wanted to press charges, but she refused. I think she was too scared. It wasn't the first or last time. I used to think he was going to kill her. One night, he ran her car off the road in the middle of nowhere and dragged her out of the car and beat her; right in front of us, again.

Over time it got to where Mommy didn't want to sleep with him anymore. I heard them argue about it. One night, I overheard an argument, Mommy was screaming and fighting back at him. I went to the kitchen to check on her. I saw he was raping her. Mommy kept telling me to go to the other room. Despite all the abuse, the obsession for him was controlling her. She went back for more.

Looking back now as an adult, I understand she needed help and counseling. I know that she had some psychological issues. When I got older, she did go on medicine. I never found out what her diagnosis was because for years she kept it from me. I think that Mommy stayed in abusive relationships because she had been so attacked on her identity. She started believing the things she was told "You are ugly" and "Nobody will want you." I believe her self-esteem was low. I think she felt guilty. She said he made her feel like everything was her fault. Eventually, she quit tending to her needs and made choices that were harmful to her wellbeing. I don't think she knew who she was anymore.

While all this was going on, she also had gotten herself pregnant by him. Twice.

She wanted no one to know she was pregnant either time with his babies. When she became pregnant with the first one and started showing, she told the whole family she was very sick and had a tumor that was making her gain weight. She got bigger and bigger. Some in the family didn't believe her, but others did and were very concerned. I remember Mamaw worrying herself about it. She even had us kids convinced.

One afternoon, Mommy started moaning and groaning. "I'm hurting, I'm hurting so bad from the tumor." I could see she was holding her legs together. I began to think she was going to die. She screamed, "Call 911! Call 911!" My shaking hands picked up the phone and dialed. Here I was, 14 years old, and didn't understand what labor looked like. I know that may sound bizarre. Looking back, I think how crazy it is that in my mind that I thought she had a tumor.

I said to the lady on the phone, "My mom has a tumor and she has been sick for a while. She is in a lot of pain. I need someone here quick." She stayed on the phone with me until the ambulance got there. I was crying because I was scared that Mommy was going to die. Then, suddenly, her water broke right there in the kitchen floor. I was so scared and confused. She was still convincing me that she didn't know what was happening and why water was coming out of her. It scared me even more. The paramedics got there and took her to the hospital.

Mamaw came and got me, Teresa, and little Billy. Mamaw wanted to go and see Mommy. But Mommy told her she was going into surgery for the tumor. Hours later, Mamaw still was waiting for Mommy to call her so that she could go and see her. Finally, she called Mamaw, but Mommy wouldn't let Mamaw see her. When Mommy went home from the hospital, Mamaw, Uncle Glen, and his wife all showed up at our house. That's when she couldn't hide the baby anymore. Mommy didn't have to explain things because Mamaw told me the truth. I was so angry at Mommy. I had been so sick with worry over her and what she had put me through. I didn't show my anger though because Mommy could get mean with us too with the hair pulling and the pinching. I knew not to cause any trouble, so I stayed quiet. I didn't like upsetting Mommy. I just wanted to have love and peace, so I did what I could.

When she got pregnant with the last one, she didn't want anyone to know again. Three months into the pregnancy, she started showing and decided to hide. She loaded all four of us kids up into her little blue Chevy Chevette and headed to a town about 45 minutes away called Beckley. That is where we lived until the baby was born. We all lived in the car just because she didn't want anyone to know she was having a baby. Most of that time, we had no money, and she didn't visit that man. I don't remember him coming to see us or meet up with Mommy.

We ate bread with ketchup on it. She would buy bread in a store. Then she made me and my sister Teresa go into McDonald's and grab ketchup packets. It was so embarrassing. It was awful having to eat that all the time. I would love to have had meat on the bread at least. Sleeping was a joke. Five of us, Mommy and us four kids, cramped in a little Chevy Chevette trying to sleep. We didn't sleep much. When she had the baby we went back home. She tried to hide the baby too, but that didn't last long. The only part that wasn't terrible was because Mommy hid from Papaw too! I didn't have to go to see him. Not one time.

Now my mom ended up with six kids, five living at home because Louise was in Texas married. One day, she stood her ground and said, "I have had enough. I can't do this anymore. He is going to end up killing me!" She sat Teresa and me down because we were the two oldest even though Teresa was still only in middle school. "You can't tell anyone because if you do, it could get me killed. But, I want you to have an opportunity to tell your friends bye. Here's what I am going to do. I am going to let you go to school tomorrow morning, and I will pick you up around lunch. I will act like I am checking you out early and I want you to act like it's normal. I need you to pack up tonight, but it needs to be just one bag each, okay? We don't have any room in the car for more than that."

To get away from that man, she packed all of us, and she drove with no idea where she was going. We could only pack clothes and leave everything else behind because what we took had to fit in the car. As a teen, that was horrible leaving everything behind.

We had to leave stuff that I had for years; the things that had become really special to me. That is how I lost my prized recorder that had Louise's message; the one she had left for me when she ran away with David. Even to this day, Teresa and I talk about it. Even though we were leaving stuff behind, we didn't care at the time. We had this relief that we were going to get away from that man. At the same time, we were sad to go away, but there was a surreal peace around it all.

Mommy drove down Interstate 77 until the gas light came on, close to an exit. We pulled into the gas station. There was a police officer there. She asked him if there were any shelters nearby and he told her about some options. We ended up at the Salvation Army's Homeless Shelter in Bristol, Tennessee. We stayed there for a while and then transferred to a nicer homeless shelter. We were there for a little while until Mommy could get a job and save money to get us a home. That's what she did, and I had renewed hope.

Living in shelters wasn't easy, but I was excited that she was far away from that man and out of the destructive relationship. She worked while we were in school. After a few months, she was able to save enough to get us out of the shelter. We went to a Church of God close by, and I loved it. I was so happy to see Mommy back in church. She did so good for a while. Life seemed normal for once.

Then she slipped back to her old ways. She started to hang around with a few men, and things went back to what I had become accustomed to. I knew I had to hold it together for the kids. I bought a car and continued to take the kids to church myself. To buy that car, I had a job as a cashier at Prime Sirloin. I worked hard and was soon, at the age 18, made Frontline Supervisor. The manager of the restaurant left there to manage the café at a new Target. She asked me to follow to be the supervisor. I did. I was grateful for the opportunity and more money. At least these guys she was partying with weren't abusive. They were drinkers and crazy, but not abusive. At least from what I saw.

If you are reading this and you know that you are in an abusive relationship and you think you don't deserve better, STOP! I am here to tell you that it's a lie from the pit of hell. You do deserve better. You have to believe it and act upon it. Abusive people do not know love or God.

1 John 4:7,8 says, *"Dear friends, let us love one another, for love comes from God. Everyone who loves has been born of God and knows God. Whoever does not love does not know God because God is love."*

People who are verbally abusive have to answer to God. Proverbs 13:3 says, *"Those who guard their lips preserve their lives, but those who speak rashly will come to ruin."*

We should never admire violent people. *"Do not envy the violent or choose any of their ways."* (Proverbs 3:31)

Victims of abuse often think they deserve the abuse. No one deserves abuse. The Bible gives scripture over and over to show that abuse is not acceptable to God.

If you are in an abusive relationship at all, get help. I have references and resources listed for help at the end of this book. No one deserves to be abused. Look at the resources in the back of the book for more information. Find your voice. Know that you can break those chains in your life for your children and grandchildren. You can be an overcomer. Your past does not define your future.

My sibling loving me over my shoulder.

Me and Mommy at the homeless shelter that were lived in at the time.

My sibling laying on my back kissing me on my bed.

Chapter 9
Daddy's Girl

Daddy's Girl

While life with Mommy was constant turmoil, Daddy was a great father, and he gave me so much hope. The situation with Louise running off was so hard on him. I remember overhearing their conversation about what they would do. As an adult looking back, I can't imagine how hard it was for him to deal with everything. His firstborn ran off to Texas, and he found out his wife was having an affair all in a matter of months. But no matter what, Daddy never let us feel that pain. He gave us memories that lasted forever.

I used to sit on Daddy's lap for hours. I always felt safe there. We'd watch football together. He would get so into the game, he would whoop and holler. We loved watching Superman and Star Wars. When he got home from work, he would get a plate of snacks; I would sit on his lap and eat with him. Daddy was the one that always did the grocery shopping. I would always go with him. He used to call me his little helper. I remember he gave me rides through the yard in the wheelbarrow. We would rake leaves up in a pile and jump in. Daddy was so much fun. From the earliest time, I can remember I was a daddy's girl. That is why the divorce was so hard on me. I was like velcro to him! Even after he moved out, he would come and see little Teresa and me after school and visit. Mommy wouldn't let him in the house, but that didn't stop him from being there for us.

Every Sunday he picked us up for church whether or not it was his weekend. They both got us on holidays. They lived so close; we would celebrate with one and then go to the other house to celebrate with the other. I got used to it, but I always wished Mommy and Daddy would get back together. He was so proud of all three of his girls, even when Louise wouldn't talk to him in the following years. He never gave up hope that he could have a closer relationship with her.

I remember when we had snow days off from school, he would take me to work with him. He had pictures of us girls all over his office. As I got older, in middle school, I walked to his house whenever I wanted. He loved being with his girls and always provided as much as my mom would let him. He would stop by the house on the way home from work. When school was out, he would take me to work with him. When he went grocery shopping, he would always go to the same store and take me with him. Everyone knew us there and would talk about me being his sidekick.

Then Mommy moved us to Bristol Tennessee. Daddy felt devastated, and so did I. I don't think I've ever seen Daddy cry so much even with Louise moving to Texas. So, when I was being taken so far away, it was an awful feeling for both of us. It was as hard for him as much as it was for me. He cried and was so hurt. He couldn't believe his little girls were being taken away from him. It crushed him to see us move away. I wondered how long I had to go without seeing him.

We talked all the time. He would call me often, and I called him every chance I got. He would come to visit us every chance he got. He never missed an event and came for school functions just to see us.

Daddy was a die-hard NASCAR fan, so he loved coming to Bristol Motor Speedway to watch the races. When I got my car, I could drive and see him on weekends too.

Graduation time came. Being young I worried that something would come up and Daddy would not be able to come. I knew he would want to. Let me say Daddy wouldn't have missed me walking across that stage for nothing even if his life depended on it. So, he took off work, drove to Bristol, and watched his baby walk across stage and graduate. He hollered and took a ton of pictures, and he told me how proud he was of me. I was so happy. Daddy paid for me to go to college. I went to Lee University, and he would make trips there every chance he got. When I got married and had Jonathan Jr., he came. He loved being involved in his grandbabies' lives as well. No distance kept Daddy away.

On the flip side, no distance kept my mom's ex-boyfriend away from my brother and sister (his kids) either. When my mom left West Virginia to move to Tennessee to get away, she was moving against court orders. Prior to her leaving, they gave Mommy custody of the kids, but he got them one weekend out of every month from Friday to Sunday. She could move, but she had to make sure the kids got to him for his visits. But once she left, she never let him see them again. He didn't know she was leaving, and he had no idea where she was. Two years went by, and he hired someone to hunt her down, and the police took the kids to him until the next court date. They gave him custody, and my mom's heart shattered. I was in college by this time, and I remember her calling me and crying. I sat on the other end of the phone and cried with her. Since they lived with him, it was impossible for me to see them too. I was heartbroken. Those babies were my babies. I loved them so much, and I had taken care of them a lot over the years.

Many fathers will do whatever it takes to get to their babies. If you are a parent, you know you would fight whatever it took for your children to be back with you. If earthly fathers are like that, how much more do you think our Heavenly Father will fight for us? If you ask your earthly father for something to drink, he will give you something to quench your thirst. You know how much we love our children and want to give them what they need and want? How much more do you think the Heavenly Father wants to give us (his children) what we need and want? He created us. He sent us to our earthly father. He knew everything about us before we were even born.

Jeremiah 1:5 says, *"Before I formed you in the womb I knew you, before you were born I set you apart; I appointed you as a prophet to the nations."* Daddy God takes care of his children!

Genesis 28:15 says, *"I am with you and will watch over you wherever you go, and I will bring you back to this land. I will not leave you until I have done what I have promised you".*

So, remember this, the next time you ask your Heavenly Father for something. He will fight for you to the end. He will never give up on you!

"The Lord will fight for you; you need only to be still."
Exodus 14:14

Photos of me and Daddy

4-16-78
Louise in front.

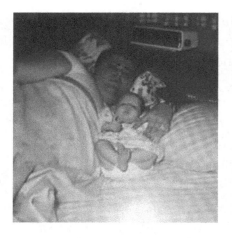

ST. PATRICK'S DAY MARCH 18

3-25-78

EASTER

3-24-78

Sisters of Secrets

Chapter 10
Escape

Escape

In June 1995, I graduated from High school. I applied to different colleges. I went to the first one that accepted me, Lee University. My thought was, "It's a Christian college, so I'll be safe there. Plus, it's only about four or five hours away from home but still far enough away." In January 1996, I packed up my things and headed to Cleveland Tennessee. I was so excited and thought it would be such an easy transition.

I wanted to escape the life of being home. Mommy followed me down in her car to help me unpack. She stayed a little while and then left. We both shed tears like crazy. I missed her from the time she pulled out of the parking lot; even though I knew I was getting away from the environment I had been in. I taped pictures of me, Mommy, Daddy, Mamaw, and my brothers and sisters all to the wall in my dorm room. I would spend hours in my room not going anywhere and not meeting any friends. I would just sit under those pictures and cry. It was confusing because this was what I wanted for so long and here I was crying. I was still so worried about Mommy because I was no longer there to protect her. I was concerned about the kids because I was the oldest at home and I had protected them. I was always there for them. That troubled me the most. The kids were so upset about me leaving and begged me to stay. The truth is, those kids were my world. I took care of them so much I almost felt like a mother figure in their life. So, that first semester, I failed every class.

Things got better, and I coped with being away from family. I met friends and got involved in a club called Pioneers for Christ. It was so neat because we would travel and do mission trips in this club and get to minister. I enjoyed it! That summer, I didn't want to go home because of how home life was. I loved my family, but I couldn't handle going back to what I had lived in. I was trying to figure out what I would do for the summer.

At the beginning of my summer break, my sister Louise and her husband David came in to visit with their four children.

While on an outing one day, I popped the question, "Can I stay with you for the summer?"

I was surprised that her answer was, "Sure!" When they left, I went with them.

That summer in 1996, on the way to Texas from West Virginia, Louise and David stopped in Louisiana at a casino to gamble. I was not aware that they took part in gambling. We were all raised up in a strict Christian home and taught that gambling was a sin. I was in shock. They explained how they loved gambling, especially Louise, and to not tell anyone in the family.

"We will park here and go in while the kids sleep. You stay here." I listened and stayed in the van with their kids in a parking garage while they went to gamble. As the night progressed, David came back to check on me.

He said, "I'm upset! Louise won't stop! I know when to stop but this is an issue with her, and I can't get her to leave. If she gambles all the money away, I don't know how we will get home." Later, they both came back. He shouted, "Louise, if you don't stop we could get ourselves in the hole!"

Louise was upset and yelled, "I am not a child! Stop bossing me around!"

When we got to Texas, I unpacked my things. It was nice at first. We played board games and watched movies and just had all kinds of fun like old times. After a couple of weeks and everyone got comfortable, strange things happened. David said things that made me feel uncomfortable. He would comment how nice my shape was, and was very flirty, even in front of Louise.

He would tease me about my high school boyfriend Brandon saying things like, "Brandon wanted to go swimming with you just to get you in a two piece to see your body and get excited." Those comments were so disturbing to me because I had never been with anyone or done anything. These comments about my body made me feel cheap.

"We're just playing around," Louise teased. They must have been able to tell I was uncomfortable. As time went on, things got stranger. One day, they were trying to come in on me while I was in the shower and I wouldn't open the door. I'm assuming it was Louise since she's the one that was carrying a coat hanger when she walked into the bathroom. She had picked the lock with it. She and David made me let them watch me shower and even get out and got dressed in front of them while they laughed to make fun of me and talk about how beautiful I was. It continued. I didn't even want to shower there anymore. To this day, I don't like taking showers.

Other things in the home were strange also, but at the time I was young and had been abused myself. I didn't see what I see now. I noticed she was very strict with the kids. Louise would set the table for a meal and call them down one at a time. They would wait for permission to sit down. After they sat down, they did not touch a bite to eat until Louise told them it was OK. She never asked if they wanted a second plate, but the kids would just sit there until

Louise would tell them they could 'get-up-and-go' back to their room. They were always stuck in their room, and the baby was always in the playpen. When I would ask if I could play with them or talk with them, Louise would say, "No, not right now." Once I asked her why, she never let me and she said she didn't want my ways rubbing off on them because I didn't believe the same as them. I felt bad, like I was the reason the kids were always shut up in their rooms. I always felt like I needed to hurry to get out of the house. Now I needed an escape from this place, too. I felt I had nowhere to go to feel safe. I was given rules just like the kids. I wasn't allowed to have friends, give anyone our address or phone number. I could only go to work and back home and be transported by Louise. I was told if I broke the rules, I would be kicked out.

Louise found out I met a friend at work and had been going with him on lunch breaks. She got so mad, she put me out on the street just like I feared. She took me to work, and when it was time to get off, she never showed up. I called and called, but she wouldn't answer. It was getting late, and the store was closing. I was scared because I had no family and knew no one in Texas. So, my boss offered to take me home with him and his wife. I said no because of all the abuse, and by that point, I trusted no one.

I walked over to Walmart after our store closed because they were open all night, and I slept on a bench there. There was an older couple that tried to take me home with them from Walmart that night, I was scared and said no. I finally got ahold of Louise, and that is when she told me I was kicked out of her house. I slept on that bench for three days. I would walk to work in the same outfit that I had on every day. The manager would let me sleep in the office until time for me to clock in.

That's when Jonathan, my friend then, my husband now, found out I was kicked out and sleeping on a park bench. He came to my rescue. His parents came, picked me up with him and took me in. They took me to Louise's house and demanded my things, and when she wouldn't give them to me, they threatened to call the police. That's when she handed them my stuff.

After staying with Jonathan and his parents, I was planning to go back to college in Tennessee. Sitting on the porch one day, Jonathan said, "I never want you to leave."

Looking back into his eyes, I responded, "I don't want to leave."

That's when he said, "I want to marry you."

"I'll marry you," I said with a smile.

From that day forward, we knew we would get married, and we looked at rings. Neither family wanted us together. Daddy was the only one that supported us. He wanted to see us get married. I hurt Daddy because we ended up getting on a bus and going to Cleveland Tennessee to the courthouse to get married. It was one big argument between Mommy and his parents. We moved into married housing on campus, and I started classes again. We quickly became pregnant with our first child which led to me dropping out.

Finally, I felt safe. However, my experiences made marriage hard. Any disagreements made me very nervous. I'd shut down if I thought he was getting upset or misunderstanding me.

If you are being abused in any way, get help. Speak out! No matter what you are told will happen if you do, still find help. There are crisis lines you can call. No one deserves abuse. Do not believe the lies of your abuser. Many times they will blame you. It's not your fault. Just remind yourself every day, who you are. Look in the mirror and tell yourself what the Bible says about you. You are fearfully and wonderfully made. You are the head and not the tail. You are above and not beneath. You are loved. You are a child of God. Just stand there and look into your own eyes, in the mirror and do this every single day until you start believing it.

My high school graduation picture. Right before leaving for college.

David holding son Jonathan, Louise, Teresa holding Jessica, me, Joshua in front of Louise, and Jennifer. The day we left for Texas when I went with them for summer break from my first year of college. June 1996.

Me and Jonathan two months before
we got married.

My husband and I with our seven
children.

Chapter 11
Destiny Faith

Destiny Faith

In 2005, at the age of twenty-nine, I had to endure one of the hardest things of my life. I was 16 weeks pregnant and so excited. I went in for a regular ultrasound just to see if my baby was going to be a boy or a girl. This was a day I thought would bring much joy to our family, but instead of finding out just if it was a boy or a girl we heard some bad news. We were devastated to hear that our baby's heart was not growing with the body. We were told at that time that I would have a miscarriage sometime. I went to my pastors and had a prayer. I went to the altar for prayer. We prayed and pleaded with God. We spoke life. We did everything that we thought we could do right. Within a few weeks, I started having complications. I started cramping and went to the doctor. They sent me home, and within a couple of weeks, I started spotting. I went to the doctor again, and they sent me home, and within days I passed a huge blood clot, and they sent me to the hospital where my water broke, and a beautiful tiny baby girl came out.

There was no life in her which was so heartbreaking! I didn't know how I could go on. What I did know is, 5 other children still needed me. I had lost her, but I still had 5 very alive children that needed me. For a couple of months after, I battled severe depression. I hardly came out of my pajamas or my room.

One day, my husband walked in to our room and said, "Babe we need you. Get up and get out of here and out of these pajamas. This is not going to bring Destiny back."

After we had a long talk, I did just that, and with prayer and support, I was able to overcome my deep depression. During this time, my husband also suffered from her death and he didn't take it well, but he was able to be stronger throughout things than me. However, I will never forget that moment when she was being shown to him, and he screamed in the corner like a little kid.

He just fell sliding down the wall into a fetal position on the floor and cried out, "No! No! Put her down you're going to hurt her!" He never held her which he later regretted.

I'll never forget that phone call when I had to tell Louise that Destiny was gone. She cried with me just like she felt my pain. She told me she was sorry. I told her the truth. I told her I was mad at her and Teresa because they were having healthy babies and I wasn't. She just sat there, but she did say she was sorry. The bottom line was, we loved each other and nothing could come between that. It wasn't Louise or Teresa's fault that I lost my baby. They both cried with me when I told them.

"I'm so sorry, Elizabeth. I wish things could be different. I wish there is something I could do," said Louise.

Teresa just felt so bad. She kept saying, "I don't know what to say Elizabeth. I love you so much and hate this."

I remember feeling so jealous of them when they went into labor.

I remember Louise telling me that she had a couple of miscarriages herself. "I know how you feel," she said while crying, "it's like losing a part of yourself."

I knew it wasn't my sister's faults that they were having a baby when mine passed away, but I was still so resentful. I tried not to be. It was hard to be excited for them, but when they had the babies, and I saw them, I did fall in love with those sweet little ones. I just couldn't help it! Of course, I cried because it reminded me of Destiny, but I loved those babies and still do today!

We don't always understand God's plan. We just have to trust that he knows best even when it doesn't seem right to us. Sometimes we just are overwhelmed with hurt that we react in a way that later we don't understand. We had 4 boys and 1 girl and was so excited for our little girl to have a sister to play with. We were hurting in so many ways. I'll never forget the feeling of going into the hospital pregnant and leaving with no baby as all the other mothers were wheelchaired out around the same time that I was to go home. They were holding their little bundle of joy, and all I felt was empty and broken! Today all we have are memories, and they aren't the best memories to have. We don't talk about her much because it still hurts so bad.

From time to time the kids would bring her up, and my husband would say, "I wish y'all wouldn't talk about it because it hurts." I caught myself doing the same thing as the kids would talk about it and I would say, "Please don't talk about bad memories."

This went on for years. Today my husband still has a hard time talking about it, but as for me, I can talk about her. Yes, it hurts, but I know that God knows best and he had a reason. I have accepted that. I also know that one day we will be together again. Loss is never easy no matter what kind of loss it is.

Loss comes and goes, but we still have to go on with life no matter how much it hurts. The way grief affects you depends on lots of things, including what kind of loss you have suffered, your upbringing, your beliefs or religion, your age, your relationships, and your physical and mental health. People react in different ways to loss. Anxiety and helplessness often come first. Sadness comes later. Feelings like these are a part of the grieving process. They will pass. Some people take a while to recover. Some need help from a counselor. With God in your life, you can eventually come to terms with your loss, and you will start to feel normal again.

There's no quick fix. You might feel affected every day for about a year or even longer after a major loss. These are some practical things you can do to get through a time of loss that has helped me.

- Express yourself. I love talking. Talking is often a good way to ease painful emotions. Talking to a friend, family member or counselor can help.

- Allow yourself to feel sad. It's a healthy part of the grieving process.

- Keep your routine up. Keeping up things such as exercise, grocery shopping, reading to the kids, etc.

- Make sure to sleep. Being emotional can make you tired.

- It's important to eat healthy.

- Avoid things that can become addictions to cover the pain, such as alcohol. It's only temporary.

- Go to counseling if you need to. Counseling may be more useful after a couple of weeks or months. The important thing is to be open to the counseling because it can help you move forward.

What does the Bible say about grief? Grief is a normal process at the death of a loved one.

Joseph was a godly man. He did not expect his father's death. Yet when Jacob died, Joseph fell on his father's face and wept. It says in Genesis 50:1, *"Joseph threw himself on his father and wept over him and kissed him."* He also observed 70 days of mourning in Genesis 50:3. *"Taking a full forty days, for that was the time required for embalming. And the Egyptians mourned for him seventy days."* It never said in the word that Joseph was unsanctified or he was saddened too much.

The Bible teaches that grief and tears are a normal response to the loss of a loved one. Jesus grieved with Mary and Martha at the tomb of Lazarus. *"When Jesus saw her weeping, and the Jews who had come along with her also weeping, he was deeply moved in spirit and troubled. Where have you laid him? he asked. Come and see, Lord, they replied. Jesus wept."* (John 11:33-35) The Holy Spirit is capable of grieving *"And do not grieve the Holy Spirit of God, with whom you were sealed for the day of redemption."* (Ephesians 4:30)

It was hard when God told the prophet Ezekiel that He was going to take his wife as a sign to the disobedient nation and he was not allowed to show signs of grief or sadness. *"Son of man, with one blow I am about to take away from you the delight of your eyes. Yet do not lament or weep or shed any tears. Groan quietly; do not mourn for the dead. Keep your turban fastened and your sandals on your feet; do not cover your mustache and beard or eat the customary food of mourners."* (Ezekiel 24:16-17) Grief is normal and proper when we lose loved ones to death. You're not more spiritual if you don't grieve.

Even though we grieve, we have hope by faith in God's promises.

Destiny Faith will always live in our hearts, and we will be together again one day.

Chapter 12
Separation And Connection

Separation And Connection

Jonathan and I had gotten married when we were eighteen and twenty-one. We brought a lot of 'junk' into the marriage from our childhoods. Mostly mine. I will say he was a nice escape, but I did love him. I was in love, but did I really know how to love considering all the abuse I had endured? The first few years of marriage were awesome. Then something started happening. I'm not really sure but a lot of arguing began. Everyone on the outside thought we had the perfect marriage because we did love each other and did everything together and did a lot of fun things together. Behind closed doors we struggled many times to get along. I think that arguing began over financial struggles as we were really suffering financially. Neither one of us had a college degree and there wasn't enough income. This stress of money was real. Eight years into the marriage we lost our child, Destiny Faith and that was very hard. We had been arguing for a few years over the finances and why we had lost Destiny Faith. The 'blame game' started. I had been taking some weight loss pills that Jonathan didn't want me to take while I didn't know I was pregnant. When we would argue he would tell me that's why we lost her. I would tell him that I lost her because of all the arguing and that he would stress me out. The blame game was serious. It just added stress to our marriage. It got worse and worse throughout the years.

Eleven years into the marriage, three years after losing Destiny, Jonathan, at age 29, became very distant with me. He would go to work, come home, get on the phone, and go for a walk while talking on the phone for hours. I figured he was having an affair. I thought, *"Who else would he be talking to on the phone for hours?"* He also became very private and we were never private in our marriage before. He would take his phone to the bathroom with him, and everywhere he went he never left it laying around like he used to and when he would go to sleep at night, he would put it under his pillow so that I couldn't get to it. Something happened to his cell phone and I called to talk to the provider to get it fixed. They told me I had to have a passcode that he had put on there and he wouldn't give it to me. At that moment, I realized that he was afraid I would get information about who he was talking to. He never talked to me anymore. When he was home, he would lay in the bedroom on the bed with the door locked. When I came to bed, he would turn the opposite direction and ignored that I was there, and if I touched him he would move.

One night I had to ask "What's wrong?"

"Nothing." He muttered.

It was like he started hating me overnight. I couldn't quit crying. I didn't understand. I just knew marriage was miserable at that time. I didn't know what to do. I asked him several times what was wrong but the answer stayed the same.

Finally, one day, he came in the dining room where we lived in Dalton Georgia to talk to me and the kids. "I've made a decision," he said, "I'm moving back to Texas. I need a break from the marriage."

"You are having an affair." I stated with certainty.

He sat there and plainly denied it while laughing. I knew what I was talking about. I told him he would never come back. He had his things packed and told me what time I needed to drop him off at the airport. I drove him to the airport which was about an hour away.

"Please don't leave me! Don't go to her and leave our family! We are getting ready to have another baby!"

I continued to cry while driving him to the airport. He even kissed me bye after I begged him to stay.

After he got out of the car to board his flight, I proceeded to drive back home. That was when the transmission went out in our Van. We lived in the middle of nowhere in rural Georgia. I had no way to the grocery store or anywhere. And we had just moved about two months before, so I knew no one. Once he got to Texas, I called his cell phone to tell him, and his reply was, "What do you want me to do about it?" We had no food, no electricity, no car, and I was being evicted from our home within a couple of weeks of him leaving. He took all the money and didn't pay any of the bills. We had six children, and I was 8 and 1/2 months pregnant with our seventh.

I was so hurt. He had promised to send money to the children and me when he got there. "My mom will send the money for the bills and take care of it," he assured. The following day, I called to check, and his mom answered the phone.

I told her about the conversation I had with him. "I never said that," she responded. "You better talk to your husband about that."

When I confronted him over the phone about sending me the money, all he had to say was, "I don't have any money to send you.

"But you promised me that you would. I am down here in Georgia with the kids, and we have no electricity, no food, and no car! What are we going to do?!"

"Sorry… I can't help it." He said flatly.

That prompted me to call an attorney for help.

A few days later, I got a call from him. "I got a call from an attorney," he said upset. "I was planning on coming home in a couple of months. I just needed a break," he told me.

"Don't you remember the conversation we just had where you said you weren't ever comin' back?" I responded.

"Well, I don't know what I want right now. Why don't you just come down here for a while and you can stay here with me at my mom's, and we will see what we can work out," he replied.

"Jonathan, I got a baby due in less than two weeks. I can't get down there," I said.

"Well, I want to be there for the baby's birth, so see if you can." His voice was convincing.

I begged my best friend Mieke to drive me to Texas, and she was livid. "I'm not driving there. He doesn't deserve you. You're going to sit here and think about this first."

I continued persuading her, so finally she caved in but there wasn't much room in the car, and it was like history repeating itself. We grabbed bags of clothes and left everything else behind just like when my Mommy had taken us away.…

When we pulled in to the driveway, Jonathan and his mom came out to the yard. His mom was cordial and said hello while hugging her grandkids. He, on the other hand, had gone over to sit at the picnic table leaving the kids to run to him. I stood there waiting for him to say something to me but that didn't happen.

"Aren't you gonna say hello?" Standing there beside him.

"Ugh... hello," he responded with a sarcastic tone.

"Okay just sit there," I returned the sarcasticness.

It was in that moment that I realized what a fool he had made out of me. He didn't want to work on it. As days went on, he wouldn't touch me or hardly even talk to me. His words and actions were so cold and mean towards me. Every night, he left to spend it with the woman he was having an affair with. This was just a devastating feeling, and it was difficult to play the role as a peace-maker for our children as they were holding on to the hope that we were all going to be okay.

Nine days after I arrived, I went into labor. Jonathan's mom drove him and me to this hospital. Usually, my children would come up on the floor with me where I would give birth, but my children weren't allowed to come up. That was hard because I missed having them around to comfort me. He was nice during the labor, but right after I gave birth, he quickly exited saying, "I gotta go." Our baby was very sick and was in NICU for several days due to the extreme stress that had been put on both of our bodies from this separation. Before driving to Texas, I had been in the hospital for stress, depression, and panic attacks and the doctors had been worried for both of us.

After I had the baby, Jonathan told me that I needed to go somewhere else to live. He admitted he had lied to me and proceeded to tell me that he only brought me out there to get his kids. "I was waiting for you to give birth so I could kick you out," he said. "I know I never want to be with you again."

Before this traumatic marriage situation, Louise and I had talked in spurs. There had been big gaps between our talking on the phone. We would talk many times and often in a run for several days and then she would suddenly quit calling. She would stop returning my phone calls, sometimes for 6 months or even a year at a time. Before my separation, it had been months since I had been able to get a hold of her or hear from her. I had been trying to call her because of everything going on especially with me being in Texas as she was only a few hours away. Shortly after arriving in Texas, I finally got a hold of her. It was just a couple of days before I gave birth. I was able to tell her what was going on and she was concerned. When I had the baby, she came to the hospital. She tried to stay close but yet keep her distance.

"I want Jonathan to take responsibility, Elizabeth," explained Louise.

Unfortunately, he didn't. During this time, she went every single day to the NICU to visit the baby and wait until he could get off the feeding tube and she could hold him. But after I got discharged from the hospital, she went back home, and she assumed that I had gone back to Jonathan's parents, which, I did… but for long.

After a few days being back at the house, he came into my room and said, "Get ready. I am taking you to the salvation army shelter." I started getting the kids' stuff together, and he said, "You're not taking the kids. You're leaving them here."

"I'm not leaving my kids here!" I cried. This caused a big argument to break out.

"Yes, you are," he said firmly.

"You aren't taking my kids to a homeless shelter." I stated.

What was bizarre about it was that he was willing to drop his newborn off there with me. He made the excuse that the baby was being nursed and he couldn't do that, so the baby needed to stay with me.

I couldn't put up a fight because his parents supported his decision. I tried to call the police but my cell phone was taken from me, and I was told by a fellow family member there, "I'm gonna throw out your cell phone on the highway."

Getting into the car, I was fighting for my kids. The kids and I were crying as he was ripping us apart. "Over my dead body, you won't have these kids!" I cried, "you won't have them long." During this time, my hair was pulled over that comment.

I had nowhere to go. I knew no one but his family that lived close by. So, he took the baby and me and dropped us off at The Salvation Army homeless shelter. I called the police, and they wouldn't do anything about it because they were his kids too.

He kept my kids away from me for a couple of months. He caused me to miss Nicole's first day of kindergarten. He and his girlfriend took her to school for the first time. That broke my heart. I also missed Ariel's second birthday. That also broke my heart. I was in a homeless shelter with a newborn baby while he was celebrating our daughter's second birthday with his new girlfriend. I couldn't even talk to my kids. I would call his phone, and he would tell me to quit calling because his girlfriend didn't want him to speak to me. I told him I wanted to talk to my kids not him and he called me a liar and said that I was using the kids to talk to him and wouldn't let me speak to them. My kids hurt just as much as I did.

To this day, I am thankful for Louise because I don't know how I would have gotten through that time in my life. She bought me a place to live and paid all my bills, even my cell phone bill every month. She helped me fight in court to get my kids back, which I successfully did. She came every weekend and took me grocery shopping. We played board games together. We would sit and talk for hours. We would go out to eat. She would take me shopping for clothes. It was amazing! I never once asked her to do any of that for me. During those talks, there were things she shared that worried me that she was getting involved in, but it was never even on my radar for child endangerment issues. This was a sister I saw first-hand fighting for me, her baby sister, to be taken care of and all of her nieces and nephews to be clothed and fed with a loving home. Maybe reading this right now will help you understand why when the news hit of her arrest, I was in complete shock. The public has made comments that I should have seen something but those 2 years of my marriage separation, I did see things. I saw a sister who stepped up to care for her sister and other children.

She never brought the kids with her to the place where I lived, but I figured it was because of everything going on. I didn't say anything at first, but after a while, because I lived there for two and a half years, I started asking her to bring them over and she would. A couple of times she brought 3 of them with her, but other than that, I never got to see any of them. She moved from Texas to California just a couple of months before I moved from Texas as promised; she was bringing the kids by the house on the way out that night. I talked to her on the phone the night they were moving. She told me they were in the van on the way. I was so excited! I stayed up all night. She never showed up and wouldn't answer any of my calls. I didn't hear from her for a couple of days. She later called, apologized, and said it got so late she changed her mind about stopping. Perhaps for some reasons she never wanted me to have a relationship with my nieces and nephews, but she has always taken care of me whether it was that little 4 year old girl or broken women.

Finally, we went to court, and the kids were awarded to me. He was granted visits, but they had to be supervised because he had taken the kids. I was so happy to have them back. Jonathan had supervised visits, so he and I did not have much communication. On one of the supervised visits, I didn't have a car, so he offered to drive the kids and me home. When we got back to the house, the kids stayed in the yard to play, but he followed me inside. After we opened the front door and entered the house, he turned my body to him and started kissing me. I didn't have time to respond; it happened so fast. "Please don't tell anyone I was in your house," he said. By this time, I knew how established he was in his relationship with his girlfriend, so I couldn't understand what he was doing. That night, he came back to revisit me.

Suddenly, I was treated like the girlfriend where he was cheating on her with me. It finally hit me that I was not going to tolerate this in my life and deserved more for myself. I put my foot down and told him not to come back to my house unless he wanted to work things out and stay for good. I didn't see him for a while after that. But one day he came to my house and sat outside my door. He showed up early in the morning after I had left for work and stayed till late in the evening. I had gone out with friends after work and had stopped off at Walmart on my way home. That was where I ran into him.

"What's up stranger?" he said with a smile. "Come take a ride with me."

"I can't. I'm with a friend." I replied back.

"I have been at your house all day waiting for you." He said.

I told my friend I was going to leave with him so we could talk. She got mad at me thinking I was stupid. He took me back to my house, and once we walked in the door, we sat down on the couch together.

"Baby, I've missed you, and I want you. You are the one I want to be with." That's what they all say, I thought to myself. Oh, now he misses me after he's gotten what he wants. Is this really happening right now?

"You have to work harder than that to get me back." I said firmly. "You don't think you can say that and just get me back, do you?"

"I will do whatever it takes. I realize what I have done and I want to make it right," he said remorsefully.

I found my voice and shared that if he ever pulled something like this again, it would be over for good. I shared what I expected, and if it didn't happen, he wouldn't be staying. I made him agree to counseling, separate, and together.

God restored our marriage in less than a year. We have now been married over twenty years.

I had been praying to God from the day he came the first time. I prayed and fasted for my marriage every day because I miss him, and that made me realize that I loved him. I told God I wasn't eating another thing and I would only drink water until he either fixed this marriage or gave me peace about letting him go. As I was laying there pounding the floor praying, I told God to let him not be able to eat without thinking about me and not be able to sleep without thinking about me. I prayed that everywhere he would look, he would see my face. I prayed that God would send a pastor to his door. I prayed that he would go to the theaters to see the movie, Fireproof, which was playing at the time.

And you know what he said to me when he came back that day? He said, "I couldn't sleep without thinking about you, I couldn't eat without thinking about you, a pastor came to my door and ministered to me, and I went by myself to see Fireproof."

He then took me on a date to watch Fireproof with him which I hadn't seen yet. I love that God restored our marriage because for over 2 decades we have been together and we are happily married. God is a restorer. He is still on the throne and answers prayer.

Looking back, the separation was the best thing for us. We began to appreciate each other once we didn't have each other. We started to really realize how much we loved each other when we didn't have each other there. We both realized how much we missed each other. We went through lots of counseling together and separately. Marriage still has its ups and downs, but we know how to handle things differently. Before the separation, he was so controlling. He didn't get his own clothes, I got them. He didn't make his own plate, I got it. He didn't ever clean, I did it all by myself. I couldn't even get him to take out the trash. For years, he didn't do anything including even laundry or picking his own socks to wear for the day. The separation made me realize that even though I missed him, I was free. He used to get mad if he thought I stayed out too long with a friend or something. I remember him screaming and yelling at me because he thought I talked to someone too long. One night, while we were separated, I went out with a friend and came home. As I was walking up the stairs to the front door, I realized, "Wow. I won't have to worry about anybody screaming or yelling at me for being gone too long."

After all the counseling and considering getting back together, I had a better voice to communicate what I expected if we were to stay together. He knew that was the only way it was going to work. I had caught that glimpse of freedom and I wasn't going back into bondage no matter how much I grieved and missed him. He knew I was serious! When he came home, he was a new man. He respected me. He helped me with things. It was so nice. We still have our ups and downs as all marriages do, but it's all in the way you handle situations. Marriage is never easy all the time. The dictionary says that love is an intense feeling of deep affection.

The Bible says in 1 Corinthians 13:4-8, *"Love is patient, love is kind. It does not envy, it does not boast, it is not proud. It does not dishonor others, it is not self-seeking, it is not easily angered, it keeps no record of wrongs. Love does not delight in evil but rejoices with the truth. It always protects, always trusts, always hopes, always perseveres. Love never fails. But where there are prophecies, they will cease; where there are tongues, they will be stilled; where there is knowledge, it will pass away."*

While we were separated, I studied this scripture. When he came home, I watched to see if he really loved me. He had failed before the separation. But when he came back, he passed. After all the counseling, making God center of our family life, and the study of scripture, our marriage has been better. Marriage can be ugly, or marriage can be beautiful. I saw this in my own life. Since neither of us had a positive marriage environment growing up, we had nothing to model. We didn't know how to do it, but what we did know is that we wanted to be different from what we grew up in. His parents divorced when he was 4. He grew up seeing fighting between his parents, and when his stepdad came into the picture, there were lots and lots of fighting and abuse. I saw Mommy going from man to man, and every man she was with was abusive except for Daddy and Bill. All I saw growing up were screaming, yelling, fighting, and abuse. On top of that, I experienced the abuse too through neglect and sexually. That's all we knew.

Jonathan's counselor shared that he had left the marriage because he had felt worthless and that the kids and I deserved more. He was trying to make himself fall out of love with me so that I would find a better man. At the same time, he had also gotten married at just 18 years old, acquired a lot of responsibility at a young age, and was diagnosed with diabetes just a couple of years before leaving the family. The overwhelm of his self-worth issues, his illness, grief over our child's death, as well as financial responsibility had caused him to want to escape just like I had wanted to in 1996.

Jonathan and I have a heart for young, married couples today because we know how the enemy can cause the breakdown in families. His personal experience of transformation is a victorious story to bring healing to other young fathers.

I am not sure how Louise handled what she went through. I wished she had gotten counseling from her childhood battles. I would have never imagined her being arrested for anything, especially something this extreme. Here she was helping me, and she needed help in ways, just ways we couldn't see. Her marriage today is now in separation and despair behind bars while mine has been strengthened.

Praise God! With God's help and our dedication, Jonathan and I learned how to set a good example of marriage for our children. Remember, you can break the chains!

"So they are no longer two, but one flesh. Therefore, what God has joined together, let no one separate."
Matthew 19:6

Jesus looked at them and said, "With man this is impossible, but with God all things are possible."
Matthew 19:26

Me and Jonathan.

Chapter 13
Dangerous Addictions

Dangerous Addictions

After seeing them gamble for the first time on the way to Texas, I knew Louise and David loved to do it. At the time, I didn't realize until how much. Over the years, even before I had moved to Texas during the time of my marriage issues, Louise would talk to me about the fights they would have over this.

Our conversations on the phone varied over different topics; many that would cause arguments. Multiple times, she would talk about going gambling with David.

"I just can't help myself," she told me, "Once I get going, I can't stop. I love the rush it gives me."

"How does that give you a rush?" I said, "I mean putting money in and knowing you might lose it all because I had never been gambling."

"Well, you've never been gambling, so you just don't understand."

Well, that was for sure. Here I was on the other side of the thought process.

"Even if I had a million dollars, I wouldn't go gambling," I said. "That just scares me. It's like playing Russian Roulette."

Maybe it was different for her because she had money from the time she married at age 16 and I had always struggled wondering how I would make ends meet.

I can't remember how many times she would tell me that she was addicted to it and laughed it off. David, on the other hand, knew when to stop with no problem. That's why it was a touchy situation between the two of them, but even that conflict couldn't bring their activities to a halt. Once Louise began drinking and going to bars, she told me, "When I drink, I just want more of it. I really can't stop then."

I think it was the first time they went to Vegas for vow renewal, David and Louise told me that they went gambling and Louise got so drunk that she could hardly stand. David couldn't get her to leave. She gambled almost all of their money. They were literally there all night. I think they said that around 6:00 am, as David was continually trying to get her to leave with concern of the money issue, she got so mad and made a scene. Louise put up the biggest fight. That's when the security guards got involved and kicked her out. They literally escorted her out. She laughed and laughed telling this story over the years. She thought it was funny after it was over. She blamed it on being drunk.

"For everything in the world–the lust of the flesh, the lust of the eyes, and the pride of life–comes not from the father but from the world."
1 John 2:16

I know they had financial issues and I would say the gambling played a big role in that. I know they filed bankruptcy very often. One day, I called her on her cell, and she answered. I could hear the noise in the background. Where are you?" I asked curiously.

"Oh, we are in the store. I wanted to get the kids some new clothes." She said.

"Oh, that sounds fun."

"Let me call you later," she quipped and hung up.

After a few hours, she called me back. "I'm sorry I had to rush off the phone. The kids were trying on clothes, and it was crazy. I'm taking the remaining kids to shop tomorrow. I have some room on my credit card that I want to use up because we are getting ready to file bankruptcy."

"Really?"

"Yeah, she continued. "The kids need some clothes, and then David and I are going to go by ourselves to get toys for them so that we have presents for Christmas and their birthdays. We stack in the garage and outbuilding so we have it when we need it."

I didn't really understand the bankruptcy process, and I asked, "They don't come and take the stuff?"

"Don't work like that," she said still holding on to her Appalachian slang that we both had. "They take your car and house but not stuff you buy on your credit card. You see, we file where we get to keep our house and car as long as the payments are caught up. Everything gets written off, and we don't have to pay for it."

After I began to understand what she was telling me, I responded, "That kinda sounds like stealin' to me."

"Well, it's not because my kids need it and I do whatever I need to do for my kids," she said. "We buy everything we want on purpose because that's a way of getting things. We are filing bankruptcy anyway, so we might as well get as much as possible before we file."

"That just doesn't seem honest to me." I said back.

"See?" she said, "This is why I don't tell you things." She got mad and hung up on me. We went for a few months not talking.

I remember telling my husband, and it bothered us. To us, it was stealing because she wasn't paying for it and she knew that. It was planned.

> *"You shall not steal, nor deal falsely, nor lie to one another."*
> Leviticus 19:11

Louise always wanted me to look at things like she did, but I just couldn't. We were so different. That is why phone calls over the years were so sporadic. She would get mad and wouldn't talk to me for months sometimes. She would even go through times of blocking me on Facebook and then unblocking me.

> *"Do not be conformed to this world, but be transformed by the renewal of your mind, that by testing you may discern what is the will of God, what is good and acceptable and perfect."*
> Romans 12:2

But after filing bankruptcy and months would pass, she would reach out again and share intimate things. The money was a real struggle for them. I remember one time just a few years ago, Louise called me to see if she could borrow some money.

"It's so expensive feeding the kids. I have a budget of $1,800 a month for food, but it's getting to where I don't have the money to budget it out," she said very concerned. "We don't have any groceries in the house, and we don't have any money,"

"I don't have any money to loan you. Go to a food bank and see if you can get some groceries." I responded.

"I have gone, and they have turned me away because they are saying that David makes too much money." She seemed very upset and even expressed that she didn't know what to do.

I felt bad, but I was so sick with Cancer at that time and was struggling financially myself. I believe that their finances were a struggle due to their choices and addictions in their life. This is why I would always question the Vegas and Disneyland trips. I couldn't understand how they could afford to drink, party, go on vacations, visit amusement parks, and gamble when they couldn't afford to feed their kids, but I felt like it wasn't my business.

When Jonathan and I went through financial challenges, we watched every penny and still to this day. We have never been able to take our kids to Disney, and our children have never seen the ocean. We always paid our bills with every dime and made sure our kids always had something to eat even if it was cereal or roman noodles which were dirt cheap. Daddy always instilled in me the principle of, "Where there is a will, there is a way." This phrase served me well over the years. I just wished Louise had caught onto this. You have to have willpower, especially when you have children. You have to look at the big picture, not just at that moment. Things can look fun, but you have to be mindful. I'm so glad I learned at an early age to look at things from this perspective.

Along with the gambling, I could see from the outside looking in that drinking and sexual addictions were taking root. I can't remember when it was, but I'm pretty sure it was around her Fortieth birthday that Louise called me on the way to a bar with David.

"Guess what I'm doing tonight?" she said excitedly. "I'm going to go drinking for the first time!"

She knew how I felt. "Louise, be careful. Don't do anything stupid that you'll regret or get in trouble for. And please don't drive after drinking," I begged.

A while later, she called me from the bar and was so drunk that I could barely make out what she was saying. She was laughing, and I could hear all the noise in the background. "I'm getting so drunk," she said slurring her words. "I'm having so much fun!" We weren't on the phone long, and I hung up concerned. Within hours of that call, she called again. "Guess what?" she said. "We have met a man, and he wants to have sex with me."

"Does David know this?"

"Yes." Her words even more slurred than the call before. "David's here right beside me. He wants me to." She went on to explain that she got married so young and that David was the only guy she had kissed or had sex with. "David wants me to do it," she said. "We're going tonight. We're going to get a hotel room and videotape it. David's going to wait outside for me and watch it later."

This was the craziest thing ever to me. I was thinking to myself, Jonathan was the only guy I had been with. We were young when we got married, but I would never do something like this, nor would I want to. It was weird and gross to me.

After she had been with the man, she told me of the experience. "Elizabeth he was rough with me. He threw me on the bed and pulled my hair and stuff. David wants me to do it again, but I told him that I didn't want to. He scared me."

The craziness went on. Exactly one year after this, David wanted to drive to that hotel and rent that same room so that he could have sex with Louise in that same bed. Louise told me they did. She later made a MySpace page that was just under her name. During this time, she would go to sex stores. She would buy role-playing clothes and post pictures of her in them while laying on the bed being vulgar. She even posted pictures of her in a bubble bath. It became crazier and crazier. She hid this from most of the family. I think my other sister and I were the only ones that knew about it. Somehow, Mommy found out and confronted Louise about it. She was so mad at Louise and they got into a huge fight about it. Louise and David then became worried about David's side of the family finding out, and they definitely didn't want that to happen. So they decided to take the page down.

"Now the works of the flesh are evident: sexual immorality, impurity, sensuality, idolatry, sorcery, enmity, strife, jealousy, fits of anger, rivalries, dissensions, divisions, envy, drunkenness, orgies, and before, that those who do such things will not inherit the kingdom of God."
Galatians 5:19-21

As I would minister to her and tell her that this wasn't a good lifestyle and she would most likely regret it one day, she would laugh at me and mock me. I told her that sometimes we do things that later come back to haunt us. I couldn't figure out how David and Louise went from strong Christian backgrounds with morals and conscience to such an ugly, nasty, and destructive lifestyle with no morals and conscience at all. It appeared they didn't take anything seriously. I also knew there were people who partied and went to bars that were successful parents, so I never thought to be concerned on that perspective. Louise said the older children were old enough to stay home and babysit, so I didn't think much of it.

It appeared to me that things were falling apart in many ways. Louise told me it was hard to keep the house clean with all the kids. She complained that the kids were messy and she didn't know what to do about it. I knew how difficult it was with seven children myself, so I knew it must be difficult with so many more. I also didn't think that it was extreme as many homes have day to day clutter with a normal, active family lifestyle.

You have to be careful in your decision making and always think about how it's going to affect you in the future. Remember to look at the big picture. This will help you to make decisions more wisely. This is what kept me from this lifestyle because I always thought of the future and the example I would set for my children.

Daddy and Louise. The last time she
let Daddy come visit.

Louise, David, and their children.

Chapter 14
Playing With Evil

Playing With Evil

During the time of my marriage separation and reconciliation, I lived in Texas for 2 and a half years. Over this time, the conversations that Louise and I had were definitely interesting. Some were normal 'sister talk' while others stretched the envelope in my comfort. Even though we lived about 3 hours from one another, she would always drive to come and see me. I was never invited to her house. She always had an excuse that it was a fun get away and that the older children were watching over the young ones for the day. She never spent the night. David came along with her to see me at the apartment where I was living alone.

In 2008, I started to see those worrisome changes. It had begun before that first drink, but it heightened after. She then started smoking. When she drank, she was more obsessed with gambling. But what became more frightening was things I didn't want to even know about from a religious perspective.

One weekend, she wanted to get my insight. "Have you ever heard of the Ouija Board?" she asked me.

"Yes, but I would never want to be around them. They're dangerous. I think they can bring out evil," I said.

"Oh, you are so silly. I could go get it, and we could play with it. It's in the trunk." She tried to convince me.

"Uh, no way. I don't want that in my house!" I exclaimed.

"Oh, good little Elizabeth. You don't want me to ask it to see if you and Jonathan are getting back together?"

"No!" I said, "I think playing with that could be demonic and I don't want you asking anything about me. Anyway, you shouldn't be playing with that. I mean, that might not be safe around your kids."

"We never do it around the kids," she said laughing, "we go do it at a hotel."

"Well, I don't want any part of it," I said.

The ridicule began. "You just love your Jesus," she teased. "I think it's cool. I have been doing some research too. I have some books on witchcraft and card reading. I even have looked into the Satanic religion and those rituals."

"What!?" I said.

"I was just curious. Lighten up," she replied, "I have already asked the board if I was going to have another baby and it has told me yes." All this really bothered me. "Louise," I said, "this isn't anything to play around with." She just laughed and laughed at me.

"Ooo, does it scare you?" she said teasing me some more.

"That stuff is very real."

"Well, that's why I bought it. I wanted to see if this stuff was real and learn about witchcraft." She went on to tell me other questions that she asked and the answers it gave her, but I can't remember what they were. I told her not to ask anything about me or my life when she was participating in that, and she told me that she wouldn't. I made her promise she wouldn't, but I don't know if she kept her promise.

Another time she visited, she asked, "Hey, you want to go to the rattlesnake festival with David and me?"

"Rattlesnake festival? What's that?" I asked.

"Oh, it's a big thing in downtown Arlington where people gather. They skin them and cook them. Women even walk around wearing them. It's so neat because there're all kinds of stuff you can buy. And they taste so good!"

"You eat them?"

"Yea! People from all over the world show up for it. It's really a popular thing."

"No thanks, I'm going to stay home," I said. She just laughed because I didn't want to go.

A few weeks later, she came to visit again, and she had an idea. "Hey, I have an idea of how you can get Jonathan back."

"Really?" I said.

"Sure! I have been reading and studying on spells we can use that will make him want to come back to you."

"If I have to do stuff like that, I don't want him back that way," I said.

"That's why I like snakes," she explained, "snakes give you power." She went on to tell me how to do witchcraft spells and what some of the actions were. Some of the things she described were very scary that I don't want to elaborate on because God really laid it on my heart and I prayed to forget these. The more she was telling me, the sicker I became. She went on to ask me to go with her, and I said no. She laughed at me, but I didn't care. Later on, I found out that she told our mom that she was attending a snake handling church. She never told me that. After the news broke on her arrest, Tricia and I went to the house in California to see where the children had been kept. One of the first things we noticed was that she had a snake statue by the door. It was a rattlesnake, and it was in attack mode. Tricia and I looked at each other and felt that there was more to this statue by the door. At the time, we didn't know what we would come to learn and we won't be able to share until after the trial is completed, but one thing I can share is, Louise was never the same after she started this lifestyle.

She would laugh at me a lot and mock me. She would call me goody two shoes. It didn't bother me. I noticed a lot of change in her life. She was drinking, smoking, partying, going to bars, practicing witchcraft, gambling, handling and eating rattlesnake, dressing and acting vulgar on Myspace, into sex practices, and it goes on and on. I was really concerned for her. I prayed for her.

"Seers will be put to shame. Those who practice witchcraft will be disgraced. All of them will cover their faces, because God won't answer them."
Micah 3:7

"Do not eat meat that has not been drained of its blood. Do not practice fortune-telling or witchcraft."
Leviticus 19:26

This next verse is why I didn't let it bother me when she laughed at me.

"Blessed is the one who does not walk in step with the wicked or stand in the way that sinners take or sit in the company of mockers, but whose delight is in the law of the Lord, and who meditates on his law day and night. That person is like a tree planted by streams of water, which yields its fruit in season and whose leaf does not wither–whatever they do prospers. Not so the wicked! They are like chaff that the wind blows away. Therefore the wicked will not stand in the judgment, not sinners in the assembly of the righteous. For the Lord watches over the way of the righteous, but the way of the wicked leads to destruction."

Psalm 1:1-6

Louise has changed so much over the years. She is not who I was raised up with. She used to be so caring and loving. That is not who Louise is today, and that is not who she was in 1996 or any of the years in between 1996 and now. I don't know why, but she could be so mean to me at times after a few years into her marriage. The things she would say to me on the phone and the way she treated me at times. I have got to say though when she quit talking to me in 2016, it didn't bother me like it used to. I did try to call her a couple of times because I did want to know how the kids were doing and things, but she wouldn't answer.

Jonathan and I reconciled and worked on our marriage. We moved back to Tennessee in November 2010. Louise and David had moved to California a couple of months before I had moved. We only had phone contact by this time. We continued the sporadic phone conversations as usual.

Snake statue on David and Louise's
front porch.

Chapter 15
Child Protective Services

Child Protective Services

What I'm going to talk about now is very difficult to speak of, but that is why I am doing it. I know that for shame to be killed, we have to step forward and not let it control us. I do know that we go through things in life to make us better and this has made me a better person and a better mom. Between the years of 2001 and 2006, I lost my children a couple of times to child protective services. Thank God they weren't taken real long periods at a time.

First of all, I want to say that my kids have never been taken for abuse. One time, CPS stepped in when we were homeless due to financial issues. The second time, my husband passed out going into a diabetic coma and my daughter a week before her third birthday couldn't wake him up. She put the dog on a leash and walked down the road looking for me while I was at a doctor's appointment. Another time they were called because the transmission went out on our van and we had no way to get our kids to and from school. That morning, I had someone take them, but they did not have a ride home. Hours after looking for someone to pick them up from school and not being able to find anyone, I decided to take my husband's small pick-up truck to get them. I had to pack all five of them in it. I got pulled over, and the police tried to call my husband and my pastor. My husband was on his way home from work by foot and didn't have a cell phone, so he wasn't reachable. There was no one to pick up the children, and there were no more options except for calling CPS to come and get them.

I write this chapter to show people that they should not live in shame. Everyone has a past no matter what your past is. It may be different from others, but everybody has dirty laundry in some way, shape, or form. For over a decade, I have dedicated to reconstructing a secure future for my family. I have focused on taking classes that were provided by scholarship on business, marketing, and branding. I have attended leadership mastermind classes, and just last year I spoke to a group of seniors getting ready to graduate from John Hopkins University. I continue to strive to break the chains of poverty for future generations in my family. I was raised in poverty, and I have to share that it is a hard chain to break because growing up it was all I knew. Getting a mentor and life coaching in my life, and committing to be better has made me stronger and more focused on how to turn my tragedies into triumph.

Shame means a painful feeling of confusion caused by the carefulness of wrong behavior. Let's see what the Bible says about shame. Everyone experiences a certain amount of shame and regret over sins committed in the past. The Bible has a lot to say about shame and regret, and there are several examples of people in the Bible who experienced these negative feelings.

Imagine the shame and regret Adam and Eve lived with after their sin. They ruined the creation God had made. Adam and Eve were in a sinless world, with pure minds and bodies, and had a close relationship with God. When they chose to sin against God, it caused sickness, death, and separation from God for eternity in hell. Everyone after that was born in sin. Thankfully, God had a plan to save us from our sins by sending his son to the cross to shed his blood. We have our own free will. It's our choice. I would think that Adam and Eve must have had regret over their loss of purity and its blessings. We know they were ashamed at their nakedness. It shows that in Genesis 3:10.

Another example in the Bible of shame and regret is when King David had an affair with Bathsheba. Her husband was killed in the battle. She had a baby boy with David. The baby got sick and died. I think David blamed himself because of his sin. For this, I believe he lived in shame. David did give his heart back to the Lord. This story is found in 2 Samuel 11.

When Peter denied ever knowing Jesus, he went and wept. I think he had shame. He got his heart right with God and became the father of the church. Luke 22:54-62 is where this story is found.

Shame should always be brought to the light by sharing it at least with someone you trust. That way, we don't let it define us. If we bury it, then we allow it to define us. Retrain your thoughts of who you are. Don't base your self-worth on what mistakes you have made. Acknowledge who you are instead of trying to think you should be someone else. Make sure that you place yourself with ones that will lift you up out of that shame.

I wrote this chapter because I did live with shame over this for years and years. The enemy would use people to bring it up to me all the time. I got so sick of walking around with this shame and guilt. I had guilt because I felt like I ruined my kids' lives. Those were lies from the pits of Hell.

We are told to confess our sins and have faith, and we will be saved. We become closer to God by praying and reading the Bible. This also increases our faith. God forgets our sins, so don't walk in shame. Look to Jesus. Put your past behind you. *"Yet to all who did receive him, to those who believed in his name, he gave the right to become children of God."* (John 1:12)

In Romans 8:1 we are reminded, *"Therefore, there is now no condemnation for those who are in Christ Jesus."* No matter how much shame is in our past, we can still have a great future. Once we give our heart to God, we walk in newness of life. God's forgiveness has overcome that shame. Another person or a circumstance can trigger shame in us. Shame can lead us to feel as though our whole self is bad, or excluded, and it motivates us to hide. Shame can lead to addictions that attempt to cover it up.

I just want to say, don't be ashamed and don't let people down you about it. Just know that the ones talking about you have dirty laundry in their closet too. It makes them feel better about themselves to talk about you. Don't get bitter towards people for talking either. Pray for them. Let your light shine.

My seven children.

Chapter 16
Losing Mamaw

Losing Mamaw

All my life, my favorite person to be with was my Mamaw. From the time I was a little girl, first, she was my Mamaw, second, a mom figure, and then my best friend. I stayed with her on the weekends a lot. I literally told her everything. She talked to me about a lot too. We used to play board games like Trouble or Sorry. We watched our favorite TV shows such as Hee Haw, Golden Girls, and Mama's Family. I would sit in the recliner beside her, and we would do word searches and see who could find the words the fastest. We used to set on the swing outside and talk for hours. Mamaw was my everything. Our favorite weekend outings were the Mall, Chik-fil-A for lunch, bowling, bingo and Tricia's parents, Uncle Carl and Aunt Shirley's house.

When Mommy took us to Bristol Tennessee to live when I was 17, one of the hardest things ever was leaving my Mamaw and Daddy. I was 17 and made sure nothing could keep me from staying close to Mamaw. I made sure I talked to her every morning when I would wake and every night before going to bed. Even while I was in college, I still spoke to Mamaw every morning and every night. I remember when she drove all the way from Princeton to Cleveland. In college, I had my own car which allowed me to visit her on the weekends constantly.

When I moved to Texas to stay with Louise for the summer, I still kept in touch with Mamaw as much as possible, but it was difficult due to the rules Louise had at her home. I had to explain that to Mamaw which was hard on both of us because we didn't get to talk as much. I was out of there as fast as I could and again I talked to my Mamaw at least twice a day as before. When Jonathan and I got married, I still kept in touch with Mamaw faithfully. We loved going to visit her. She and Jonathan quickly became close and loved each other. Nothing would ever keep us apart.

Around 2006, Mamaw started showing first stages of Dementia. I don't remember exactly when but Mamaw was still in her right mind in the early stages of Dementia and she asked Mommy to live with her to take care of her because she knew eventually she wouldn't be able to care for herself. I thought that was a good idea. During those times of her illness, I still talked to Mamaw every day at least two times if not more. Mamaw's condition worsened and worsened over the years. She had several falls that caused hip problems which caused her to be in the hospital several times. Eventually, it started getting hard on Mommy to take care of Mamaw. It got to where Mamaw wore diapers and pretty much couldn't do anything for herself. I remember this being very stressful for Mommy. Mamaw still remembered me though when I would call or visit.

Then the call came from Mommy. She told me that the doctors said Mamaw didn't have long to live. They gave Mommy the option of having hospice at home or putting Mamaw in a hospice home. Mommy didn't want Mamaw to die in the house, so she chose to put Mamaw in the hospice home. Jonathan, the kids, and I would pack up every other weekend (when he didn't work) and head to West Virginia to where Mamaw was living. She always knew who I was even though she hardly knew anyone else. She used to cry and beg me not to leave. Ever since I can remember, Mamaw would always hold my hand and she would do it uniquely. She would put my hand between both of her hands so that one of her hands were on top and one of her hands on the bottom of my hand, and she would just hold it like that all the time while we were sitting there talking or whatever. When I would visit her with the kids and Jonathan every other weekend at the hospice home, she would hold my hand like that for hours, and when I would say I had to go, she would cry and beg me not to go.

I specifically remember the last time I saw her alive. She cried and cried and begged me not to leave and kept holding my hand like that and I promised her I'd be back in two weeks on the weekend, but she still didn't want me to go. I didn't want to, and I cried all the way home. It was almost the weekend to go and see Mamaw again, and I got a phone call, and it was Mommy telling me that Mamaw had passed. I was so close to making it back to see her again as I promised. I didn't make it. I was devastated that I wasn't there to say goodbye. Jonathan, the kids, and I headed to West Virginia to be with the family. There, I got to see my cousin Tricia after all the years apart. But Louise wasn't there, and I just couldn't understand how she could miss the funeral service.

Louise was always close to Mamaw when she was growing up, very close like Mamaw and I. When Louise married David, something happened, and she didn't stay in touch with Mamaw anymore. She didn't keep in touch with any of the family really. She did stay in touch with everyone up until her fourth child was about one year old which was that summer of 1996. She did talk to Mommy from time to time, but I figured that she still loved Mamaw. As close as they were growing up, everyone was shocked at Louise not making it to the funeral. I will never forget how everyone reacted to that. My husband and 2 oldest sons were pallbearers.

This was one of the hardest times of my life. I always dreaded the day that we would have to lay Mamaw to rest. I was hurting so bad. My mind kept playing over and over on how Mamaw did not want me to leave that last time I saw her and how I promised I would be back and she didn't make it until my next visit. How do you go on in life after losing someone you love so much? I took Mamaw's death harder due to the duration and closeness of the relationship. In deep moments of grief, I would just think about what all I learned from her. I remembered the good memories I had and the impact she had on my life. My sister Teresa and I love sharing stories we have of her still to this day. This brought comfort knowing that her time alive was filled with family, love, and good times. I look at pictures often and talk about those wonderful memories with my family. My sister Teresa and I comforted each other during the first stages of grief. It was so hard for both of us. I spent a lot of time praying and reading the Bible to find comfort. We remembered the good times that we shared with Mamaw. We reminisced about the times we laughed and the silly things we did together. Teresa and I talked on the phone a lot after her passing which gave us both a tremendous amount of comfort. But it was different with Louise. She wouldn't talk much about it. I don't really understand why. She did say how much she loved Mamaw and she had great times with her but that's it. She would not elaborate on it. I wonder if it bothered her that she wasn't there and she did miss Mamaw? Maybe that's why she wouldn't talk much about it.

Mamaw taught me to cook stuff from scratch, as far as meals but she taught me to make fudge, and after she passed, I found myself making this more often. She taught me to crochet. I found myself wanting to do this more. Things we did together a lot like bowling, eating at Chick-fil-A, and going to the mall, I suddenly liked doing more often. I began to remind myself that she is in a much better place and happy. She's not suffering anymore. I know I will see her again one day!

Jonathan, me, and Mamaw.

Mamaw and Mommy with my kids.

Me and Mamaw.

Me and Mamaw.

Mamaw with my six oldest kids.

Mamaw, me, and Mommy. Mommy holding Ariel (my daughter) and Nicole (my other daughter).

Sisters of Secrets

Chapter 17
Loving Mommy

Loving Mommy

My relationship with my mom has been hard for others to understand. It's hard for me to understand. I remember Mommy being loving to me like any other mother when I was small but my mom was very involved in church and seemed to love the Lord very much and taught us about God. She played the piano and sang. We went to church every time the doors were open. I know she believed in God and trusted God because she prayed a lot about things and went for prayer. I do remember good times with her though. We used to play jacks, board games like Operation, Yahtzee, and Sorry. I also remember playing card games with her. I remember her tickling me, singing funny songs, and doing funny things like telling me stories to make me laugh too. It was really confusing to me how she would down-talk me to everybody else, but behind closed doors, she acted as if she was a regular mother that loved her child. I always wondered if she suspected that I had told Daddy that night to pick up the phone to learn about the affair, which led to the divorce.

Those times after she and Daddy divorced, it did become worse. When she was so desperate for money, it's hard to say the truth of how she was prostituting her own kids out to my Papaw (her dad). She didn't know that I noticed what she was doing because I was so young. And there were those times that she would lock us in her car by ourselves in the middle of nowhere in the dark. She would go and do whatever she needed to do and then come back. That was pretty scary for a little girl like me. Either way, I was terrified, so there was no winning or losing whether she left us home or took us with her. As an adult, I had nightmares and had to go to counseling for it. I love my brother and sister. They were like live baby dolls to me. I took care of them a lot. Mommy was always into so many things that there were times I even took them to school with me.

As I got into my teen years, I wanted to wear shorts, not short shorts, just regular shorts, wear makeup, wear jewelry, and stuff just like all the other teen girls. One day, I asked if I could wear some things and she bit back at me, "You're acting like a slut! You're stupid, and I didn't raise you to be like that." That really confused me considering her lifestyle. She wouldn't ever tell me sorry, but within an hour or so, she acted like nothing ever happened and she loved me again. The older I got, the more of a wedge I felt between us. She would even get mad at us about wanting to go to church with Daddy, and I remember her screaming at me while driving down the road and driving crazy when she would get mad; it just wasn't right. So, once again, it was like I was the mom of all the kids again. I took them anywhere I went. We went to church together. I made sure they were all taken to school. If I went to the store, I would take the kids with me a lot of times because Mommy wouldn't be there to watch them. It was a very destructive relationship but I love my mom so much, and I can't explain it.

The time had come for my high school graduation. I moved on to Cleveland Tennessee to go to Lee University. I found myself living in a lot of guilt for leaving the kids at home without me. I was concerned about them not being taken care of. I also worried about Mommy and felt guilty leaving her because of her dangerous ways. I would go home to visit her on weekends, and she would start fighting with me out of nowhere. I remember one time going home and a friend going with me to visit, and Mommy got so mad about something that she put her fist through the window. I can't even remember what it was about, but she got so mad. Most likely, it was nothing like so many times. I was so embarrassed. The older I got, the better the relationship got. As she got older, she quit that lifestyle and started going to church, playing the piano, and singing again. She had hit rock bottom and turned her life around. Our relationship started getting much better. She got back into the church, stopped with her destructive lifestyle, and was singing and playing piano in the church again. I talked to my mom on the phone every day and actually twice a day because she would call me every night after the eleven o'clock news and we would talk for hours. I would tell her everything.

You think I would learn. Once again, I was hurt to find out that she was telling everything I would tell her to others in the family, and it would get back to me, but she would lie about me and exaggerate everything or make everything look bad even if it was good. I just wanted a normal loving mother relationship so much that I kept putting myself in that situation. I would ask her about it, and she would deny it, and I would still tell her everything. I mean, I thought she was doing well. She appeared to be living a Christian life. So I just kept talking to her or and acting like I never heard anything about her talking about me. I don't understand to this day how I kept putting myself through that over and over. In 2013 and 2014, I prayed for God to somehow fix our relationship and make it good. I was power of attorney over my dad, and he had become very ill with his dementia to where he could not live by himself anymore. I was forced to go to Princeton West Virginia to live for about a year and take care of my dad's estate and everything until I could bring him home to Cleveland Tennessee with me. I was so mad. I remember praying to God why this happened. I did not want to go back to Princeton West Virginia to face all the horrible memories of my childhood. I couldn't see it, but God was fixing my relationship with my mom.

The whole year and a half I lived there, I was with her almost every day. We were eating lunch together, eating breakfast together, and going to the kids' school functions together. Of course, even when I lived in Cleveland Tennessee before this, she would always drive to

Cleveland to see the kids in plays, or go to grandmother breakfast with them and different things. She did love her grandkids. I was able to buy her groceries if she needed it and help her with bills when she needed it. I was able to love her like I always wanted to do, and in return, she was able to be there for me. For once in my life, I felt happy with my mom and I. God was answering my prayer. Even though I hated living in Princeton, I love being close to my mother. The kids got to spend the night with her and got to go to church with her and sing with her in church. My kids got so attached to her.

Little did we know that three months after we moved back to Cleveland Tennessee after watching my mom stand in the driveway and beg me not to leave, she was going to go to heaven. I remember not being able to get a hold of my mom and thought it was odd, but sometimes she did that and then she would call me back. So I didn't think much about it. I remember telling Jonathan, my husband, that I was worried about Mommy and he said, "I wouldn't worry about it. You know she does this sometimes."

The next night, I got a text from Teresa, my sister, asking me if I heard anything yet.

"What do you mean?" I asked. She then called me.

"Billy's coming over, he needs to talk to you." Sounding upset.

Then I got a phone call from Billy saying he was coming over because he needed to talk to me. It was an emergency. They said they felt like this was something I needed to be told face-to-face. I immediately felt like it was Mommy. I kept telling my sister Teresa to please tell me it's not Mommy. She just told me she had to go and Billy would be at my house in a few minutes. Teresa was crying. I told my husband Jonathan that I felt like there was something wrong with Mommy. Jonathan said, "It's not your mom." A little after 11:00 pm, my brother Billy pulled up to my house and asked me to go out on the porch with him so that the kids wouldn't hear what he had to tell me. He told me Mommy was on life support and wasn't expected to make it through the night and that him, Teresa, and I needed to pack up and head to Princeton.

I remember just screaming, "No!" He hugged me and tried to console me as he was crying too. I started packing my bags and Billy left and said he would be back for me. Jonathan was taking the kids to friends' houses trying to find places for them to go so that he could follow me up the next day. He went to take one of our daughters to her friend's house and I remember the three youngest were already gone and it was just me and the three oldest at the house. I went into the kitchen and I was screaming out to God, "Why God, why would you make our relationship so good and then just take her?" I was so mad. I prayed and prayed for God to save her. I told God that if for some reason he had to take her and he chose not to heal her here on earth to please give me one last chance to talk to her. I remember Billy, me, and Teresa driving up there and we got a phone call saying that Mommy had come to and she was breathing a little on her own and that they may be able to turn her life support down a little. They said that she was making a turnaround, but she still had a long road ahead of her. We were so excited. Once again he answered my prayer.

We arrived at the hospital. We went in one at a time and talked to Mommy alone while we had a chance. We were able to have time alone with her and say whatever we needed to say as we all had our problems with Mommy over the years. I will never forget that conversation I had with her. With tears streaming down my face as I write this chapter. I remember asking Mommy if she was scared and she shook her head no. I asked her if she was hurting or in pain and she shook her head no. I asked her if she was glad that

I was there and she shook her head yes with a smile. I asked her if everything was OK between she and I, and she shook her head yes and squeezed my hand with a smile. I asked her if she forgave me for everything if there was anything she needed to forgive me for and she said yes. That's when I told her that I forgave her for everything. She had life support down her throat, so obviously, she couldn't talk but she would move her lips and I was able to see what she was saying, so she could confirm what she was saying by shaking her head. She mouthed I love you to me and I asked her if that was what she said and she shook her head yes. The nurses and doctors at that time thought that she was going to pull through but they did tell us that she had a long road ahead even if she did. That night, her stomach swelled up and they had to do another emergency surgery on her. They were worried. We were all worried because she was too weak for the surgery. Going into surgery we didn't have much hope of her pulling through. I remember her being so scared to go into surgery. She didn't want to have it done but had no choice. The surgery went great and we were so excited. They told us she was sleeping and she needed her rest and to go back to the hotel and come back tomorrow. So we left and went to the Waffle House to eat and after that we were going to go back to the hotel room. We had just ordered our food and got our drinks and the phone rang which was about 20 minutes after we left the hospital. They said Mommy had crashed and this time they really thought she would never pull through. We rushed back up to the hospital and surrounded her bed once again with her lifeless.

We cried, prayed, cried, and prayed till we didn't know what else to do. We were told that her brainwaves were gone. Two days later and we pulled the plug. Teresa was holding one hand, Billy was holding the other hand, and the rest of us gathered around her on her bed holding on to her legs and feet. I remember having my hand on her leg right behind Billy, and him asking, "Do you want up here for a minute?"

"Yes," I said full of tears and we switched places. I was holding her hand and kissing her forehead when she took her last breath. I will never forget that last gasp for breath. It has been a nightmare for me.

I miss those midnight talks. I would give anything to bring her back. No matter what Mommy did to me, I loved her so much. I always felt that her actions were due to all of the abuse she experienced as a child, and she never got help to cope with it. I know that Papaw molested her over and over. I always felt like Mommy did her best; the best she knew how. Even when she let Papaw molest us for money, I feel like she was justifying it as she needed money to feed us, pay the bills, and justified it as it was the best for us. I'm not saying what she did was right because I know it was very wrong and that's why I got help and broke the chains for my children, but I'm saying in my mom's sick mind, she thought she was doing what she needed to do. I think laying in that hospital bed, she had a lot of time to think through and I think that she made things right with God.

Mommy feared hell. I have peace that Mommy gave her heart to the Lord. If this chapter speaks to you, just remember you only have one mother. Try to make things right and do what's right. Pray for them instead of hating them for what they put you through. The Bible says to honor your mother and father it doesn't say to only honor them if they do you right. One thing I can say is, I honored my mother and father until death.

When Mommy passed away in February 2016, Louise called me on the phone and told me I shouldn't go to her funeral and shouldn't have been at the hospital. She said that my other siblings told her that Mommy didn't want me there and I shouldn't do something against Mommy's will. Mommy and I were close at that time. I moved to West Virginia to take care of my dad for almost 2 years.

During this time, Mommy and I spent virtually every day together. So, when Louise said these things to me, my heart hurt. I thought to myself, "Mommy's dead and gone. Why was she even saying this for?" I wouldn't dare tell a sibling that even if it was the truth. At that time, I told my husband that Louise was full of the devil. He told me he had been trying to tell me that for years. She had become so mean to me and hurtful. She decided she didn't want to talk to me anymore and was never gonna talk to me again at that point because I went against Mommy's wishes.

What really gets me is that when Mommy was on her deathbed, she wanted to see her grandkids one last time, and Louise wouldn't do it. She asked to at least talk to Louise, and she wouldn't talk to her either, neither did she come to Mommy's funeral. She went to Vegas instead. She said that she didn't have the money to come and that Vegas was already paid for. I don't know what to believe. But I know I wouldn't have missed either one of my parent's funeral for nothing in the world.

"Honor your father and your mother, so that you may live long in the land the Lord your God is giving you."
Exodus 20:12

Me and Mommy.

Teresa and me kissing Mommy.

Me and Mommy.

Mommy and me with my kids.

My husband Jonathan, me, and Mommy.

Me and Mommy.

Mommy and I.

Mommy holding my son Jacob, my son Jonathan Jr. to the left, and my son Joseph to the right.

Mommy with my oldest three children,
Jonathan Jr., Joseph, and Jacob.

Chapter 18
Good Bye Daddy

Good Bye Daddy

It was 2011 when my dad told me, "I think I need to go to the Doctor. I can't seem to remember things." Daddy said it so many times but wouldn't go. He hated going to the Doctor, but Teresa and I kept pressing him until he finally went. After a few days, he called me up and broke the news to me that he was in the first stages of Dementia. I can't remember what I said at that moment, but I just remember crying and crying. One of Daddy's favorite things to do with Teresa and me was to reminisce, so the thought of him losing his memories was heartbreaking.

When I got married, Daddy cried. He loved Jonathan though. He told me one time that Jonathan was the only son in-law that he liked. He said that something was weird about David because Louise couldn't talk or see the family anymore and he said any 23-year old that would run off with a 16-year-old isn't any good anyway. Jonathan and Daddy had a strong bond. It was neat because they were so alike. They had the same favorite movie, liked the same food, and liked the same sports. They both thought highly of each other.

One day, he called me up and wanted me to come and talk to him. "You know that Louise is the oldest and normally the oldest would handle things like this, but you know how Louise has been. She hardly talks to me and never visits. Shoot, it's been 15 years since she's come home," he said with sadness in his tone. "You and I have always been close, and I really would like you to be my Power Of Attorney. You are here, and she lives on the other side of the country with all those kids, so it would be hard for her to come and take care of anything."

"Sure Daddy. I will," I said getting up from the table to hug him. Shortly after I left, he called her and told her that and told her he didn't want her to be offended but he was going to ask me to be his Power Of Attorney since I was the next oldest. After that, we went and completed the paperwork.

When Daddy's illness started to decline, and I was taking care of him, Louise began to accuse me of stealing his money and stuff. She called Mommy, my sister Teresa, my Aunt, and others bashing me and saying she knew I was stealing Daddy's money which I was not. It was so hurtful. I had proof of where funds were going because I was paying his nursing home with it. It took his whole monthly check to just pay that until I moved him in with me and then I had an attorney watching over his expenses. I was hurt that she would accuse me of this, and it went on for years until he passed.

He was completely bedridden and could only eat soft stuff. It was so hard seeing him this way. He asked me over and over to call Louise to let him talk to her, and I did, but she wouldn't answer the phone. I finally left her a message that Daddy was in hospice, and he could go anytime, and he wanted to talk to her thinking she would hear the message and call. I also sent her a text so that I knew between both of them she would get the message, and still no call. He kept asking me to try again because he had something to tell her. When she would never answer or call him back, he finally with tears streaming down his face said that she doesn't want to talk to him. That broke my heart. My sister Teresa even stood by my dad's bed at my house and tried to call Louise for Daddy, and she wouldn't answer her either.

In 2014, he got to where he couldn't take care of himself anymore. I had to go to West Virginia to take care of him. I stayed about a year and a half so that I could get his home sold and auction off some of his personal property so he could come back to Tennessee to live with our family. During this time, Jonathan came as often as possible as he had a job there. I took care of my Daddy. It wasn't easy, but it was rewarding. He got to where he wore diapers, had to be fed, and pretty much couldn't do anything for himself anymore. I never got any sleep. It was so rewarding though to be able to be the one taking care of him and knowing he was well taken care of. It was also rewarding getting to give back to him for all those years he was raising me and taking care of me. In 2016, it had come the time where he needed hospice.

When Daddy was on his deathbed, he asked several times to talk to Louise, and she wouldn't answer. Daddy would cry saying, "I guess she doesn't want to talk to me." She was aware that I was trying to convince her to talk to him because I messaged her privately on Facebook, messaged her by text on her phone, I left voicemails on her phone, so she clearly knew that Daddy wanted to talk to her. She wouldn't answer me. She later told me the reason she wouldn't answer was because she thought I was using that as an excuse to talk to her and she was mad at me and never wanted to speak to me again. What I believe now is, she knew Daddy wanted to talk to the kids on Skype and she didn't want to have to tell him no.

When he passed in May of 2016, just three months after Mommy, she wanted me to send all kinds of stuff from his funeral to her because she refused to come to his funeral as well. I was so upset and told her, "No, absolutely not." She didn't care enough to pick up the phone and talk to him, so why should she care enough to want some stuff of his? This was my mind and heart hurting terribly from all the pain that had built up over the years of losing Mamaw, Mommy, and now Daddy. I didn't have a sister anymore. She was in her own world it seemed. When she didn't come to his funeral, we got into a huge fight over this. She even sent her in-laws to the hotel where we were staying for Daddy's funeral to scream in my face about it. I told them exactly how I felt. I told them she wouldn't get anything after the way she treated my parents and wouldn't talk to them. I was so hurt for my parents.

I am so grateful my parents and my Mamaw weren't here for this nightmare and had to face what Louise has done. Up until 2 weeks after her arrest in January of 2018, I had not heard from her at all. She even blocked me on Facebook. Two weeks after being arrested, she started calling me from jail wanting to talk.

Daddy passed away on May 15, 2016, just three months after we lost Mommy. Oh my goodness, I had never hurt so bad in my life!

My cousin Tricia was there for me for both of my parents' death. I remember her talking to me for hours both times, and she called to check on me often. She helped me get through. I had to do everything by myself. I did Daddy's obituary, planned the funeral, and everything by myself. I sat that night and listened to music all night to pick the perfect songs for Daddy's funeral. I wanted Daddy to have the best funeral ever because he deserved it and it was my last time to honor him. It was hard planning all of that myself, but it again was an honor. I would do it all over. I asked Teresa to do a eulogy because I was doing one and she said yes. Daddy loved us reading letters we wrote to him. I knew we had to do a eulogy for him because he would have been so proud. Again it was not easy for Teresa or I to get up there and read those, but it was an honor. I honored my dad until death. I miss Daddy like crazy. It's not the same without him. Losing him was so hard on me. If you still have your dad, make sure you spend every minute you can with him. They aren't around forever, and you only have one dad. I miss my Daddy like crazy!

There was one time, and I can't remember exactly when she called me after Daddy's death and told me since Janna, her youngest baby, the one that's two now, was born with red hair, she bought a whole bunch of aunt shirts for her to wear regarding me. She told me that since I upset her that I'm never going to see Janna in them and that she wouldn't send me those pictures and that she was going to make them for Teresa instead. She tried to hurt me. Since all this has happened, I asked Teresa about that, and she said Louise did call her and told her that same story and sent the pictures of Janna in the shirts and told her they were for her now since she and I were not on talking terms. She said Janna would never have a relationship with me. To be honest, none of the kids have ever been able to have a relationship with me, so I don't know what she meant by that. She has never allowed any of us in the family to have a relationship with any of her kids.

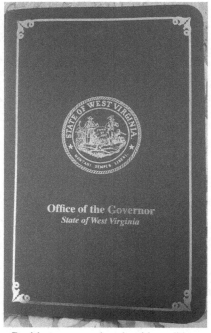

Daddy was very involved in politics. The Governor's secretary showed up to Daddy's funeral to find me and give me one of these for each kid and grandkid of Daddy's in memory of him. This is the front.

This is the inside of the Governor's memoriam that was given us kids and grandkids.

Picture I bought for daddy's funeral
from Jonathan, the kids and I. To
Daddy/Grandpa

This is hanging in the office that was
Daddy's office at work. The guy that
has that office now put that up in
memory of daddy and invited me up
there to see it.

Roses I bought for Daddy's funeral
from Jonathan, the kids and I. To
Daddy/Grandpa.

Daddy's grave.

Each one of Daddy's kids: Louise, me, and Teresa with our husband's and kids. I wrote a message to him on mine. Daddy loved pictures and his kids and grandkids. So I buried him with these. That's the lid of his casket.

Daddy's favorite sport.

Daddy was so proud. Even his car said Democrat.

Daddy was into politics and active in
the Democratic Party.

Daddy's NASCAR collection. He got to meet Jeff Gordan and
ride with him before a race. He talked and talked about that.

Chapter 19
Battle For Life

Battle For Life

My husband and I got married 1997and he was a healthy young man. About 5 years into the marriage, he began to vomit every day of his life. He went years not knowing what was wrong with him. We saw doctor after doctor. About three weeks after I gave birth to our daughter Nicole, he got very ill. He was talking about things that didn't make sense almost like he wasn't in his right mind. He was rushed to the hospital to find out for the first time that he was a diabetic. When he got there, his sugar was over 1200. They said he was on the verge of going into a diabetic coma. They actually told me that they didn't even know if he would make it through the night. Of course, he did, and he's still with us today by the grace of God.

He was in the hospital for a long time. Our lives changed. One of the few things I did different was to stop frying food. This was just the start of this brutal disease. No matter how hard we tried to do what was right for his health, it just seemed to worsen and worsen, and the diabetes seem to be taking control of his health at such an early age. Since then, he has suffered diabetic coma twice, DKA (A serious diabetes complication where the body produces excess blood acids (ketones), Acidosis (Ketoacidosis). When you have diabetes and don't get enough insulin and get dehydrated, your body burns fat instead of carbs as fuel, and that makes ketones. Lots of ketones in your blood turns it acidic, which causes Pancreatitis (An inflammation of the organ lying behind the lower part of the stomach (pancreas). There were lots of infections in his body which is so hard to fight off when you're a diabetic. There are bone infections which have led him to losing a toe on his right foot and over half of his left foot. He has had a heart attack. He has kidney failure and heart failure. He has survived sepsis twice and so much more. Sepsis occurs when chemicals released into the bloodstream to fight an infection trigger inflammation throughout the body. This can cause a cascade of changes that damage multiple organ systems, leading them to fail, sometimes even resulting in death. The doctors have told me so many times he was going to die. Every one of these situations is life-threatening.

This man is a walking testimony. His health has not been an easy road for any of us including the kids. It has been so hard for him to hold a job for years. He has been judged so badly over this by people that don't know us personally because they don't know the seriousness of his sickness. We have struggled severely financially over his sickness and have even had to file bankruptcy on three different occasions. I've never seen a man fight so hard for his family in the midst of his own struggle. He would lose a job because he would end up in the hospital and go right back to work the next week.

He knew he wasn't supposed to work, but he also knew that we had bills and kids. He tried so hard to support his family. In 2016, my husband was in the hospital for three months fighting for his life with sepsis, bone infection, and some other complications. He went from the hospital to a nursing home for three months. Then from that nursing home back to the hospital for one month. And from the hospital to home health. We were excited about him being home until 2017 sepsis hit him hard again with a bone infection. Again we didn't know if he was going to pull through. Once again he was hospitalized for a long time then back to the nursing home, back to the hospital, back to the nursing home, and from there back home. He has filed for disability over and over, over the years and finally got approved winter of 2017. My husband is now in a wheelchair at 38 years old with only one foot.

I have watched my kids cry at night not knowing if their father was going to wake up the next morning. My sixteen-year-old son Jacob was riding with me in the car one day and he was looking out of the window with tears in his eyes and told me his biggest fear is losing his dad. This broke my heart. I was lost for words. I've never seen my kids pray so hard in their lives, especially Joseph and Nicole as they did for their dad. This was hard on every one of us. Jonathan would cry on the phone with me. He missed being home with the kids and me. He has really struggled with his faith through all of this because he can't understand why God hasn't healed him. I have even seen him angry at God. Especially when he lost his foot which has been one of his biggest fears. He really doesn't know how to feel. Even though he was angry and would say things like, why hasn't God healed me and answered my prayers, he would look at me and say, please pray for me with tears in his eyes. He continued to hold on to God and stay in church and has been a trooper through all of this. I couldn't imagine being in his health condition at his age. I know that one of his biggest fears is not being able to finish raising his children. He talks about how his dream is to see all of them graduate and make something of their ife and to be able to enjoy grandchildren one day.

I'm so proud to be his wife. He is one of the strongest people I have ever met. He is in chronic pain all the time. He says his insides hurt constantly. He has a stomach issue called gastroparesis caused by his diabetes to where his food does not digest and stays down. He throws up after every meal, sometimes several times. Even though he's in chronic pain all the time, he makes a way to joke and enjoy his children and me. I have seen him cry in pain and tell me it hurts so bad and no one understands. He's such an inspiration to so many and doesn't even realize it. He has suffered depression issues from all this also. Some days he may be tempted to pretend he never received his diagnosis. He knows facing his diagnosis head-on is the best way to cope. He knows he needs to try to manage the things in his life that are within his control.

He does his best at this by controlling what he eats and drinks and taking his medicines. He may not be able to control certain aspects of his disease, but he can choose to eat healthy meals, take medications as prescribed and choose to surround himself with positive people. Being diagnosed with a life-threatening terminal disease has triggered feelings of fear.

My husband is not the only one that has had to battle for life. I had battled for life on several occasions and fought hard and won the fight when no one thought it was possible. Jesus looked at them and said, *"With man this is impossible, but with God all things are possible."* (Matthew 19:26)

It started with the heart condition I was born with that I talked about at the beginning of the book. Then into my early adult years, I kept getting blood clots all throughout my body which is dangerous, and after a lot of testing, I was diagnosed with Protein S Deficiency Disorder. People with this condition have an increased risk of developing abnormal blood clots. In 2008, the same year my husband left, I became very ill slowly. I had been to the doctor over and over. A lot of people accused me, especially Jonathan's family, of acting to get attention. I began to overlook the illness for this reason over the next couple of years by not letting others see me sick and not showing my pain to even my husband or children. By 2011 I was getting worse. It was getting to where I couldn't really hide any longer. I went from hospital to hospital and doctor to doctor. No one could find anything wrong with me. I began to pass out and fall a lot. It was getting hard for me to drive. I was scared that I was going to die and no one would know why. I started bleeding like a menstrual period but much heavier. I bled every day, and no one still knew why although I had to get blood transfusions. Finally, a doctor said, "I think you may have the last stages of cervical cancer." They sent me another doctor, and they said, "No, you have endometriosis." Then after another doctor got a hold of some test, he said, "You have a tumor in your uterus." I then had surgery and had my uterus removed only to hear the "C" word. Cancer! Exactly 30 days after my surgery, I was so sick and woke up in the middle of the night in excruciating pain and couldn't even dress myself. My husband dressed me and rushed me to the hospital but by the time we got there I passed out and didn't remember anything until I woke up and saw them rushing me off to surgery as my husband was crying and kissing me bye. I was scared and to out of it to find out what was wrong and that's all I remember until I woke up in a room later after surgery to find out my appendix was about to burst and they had to remove them quickly. I was starting to have a lot of pain urinating. They were doing all kinds of test to see why. It was the worst pain ever. They said that 97 percent of my urine was blood. So, of course, that wasn't good news. That is a sign of cancer in the bladder.

I underwent all these tests. I was told that there was not much hope. I remember the day after fighting and fighting for my life like never before, going on two years sitting in that office holding my husband's hand and waiting for the news of whether cancer is still showing, smaller, bigger, or gone. We felt as if we couldn't breathe. It was so quiet in that room. The doctor came in with a smile on his face and said, "You won!" I remember looking up and saying, "Thank you God" with tears streaming down my face! I'm not the one that won that battle, Jesus did! Everyone wants to know my secret to the love and forgiveness I have; it's simply Jesus!

This is all I can share right now about this time in my life. It's very hard for me to talk about. Later I might write a book on just this. During this time, Louise was talking to me on the phone pretty regularly to check on me and even cried often out of worry of losing me. There has never been a doubt in my mind that Louise didn't love me!

More than ever, it is vital for us to surround ourselves with positive and supportive people. If you are going through something similar, try to find small things that you can enjoy every day, and set realistic short-term goals for yourself. Even small goals such as lunch with a friend, or going to the store and buy yourself something. I try to live as normal as possible daily. I try to keep Jonathan's mind off of his condition. He has good days and bad days. The kids and I try to support him right where he is at. I want to say, though there are times that he does struggle with his attitude about this like we all would, but overall, he has had the BEST attitude ever. I love this man of God and how he has shown our children so much strength and faith through all his pain and struggle. Jesus tells us that we will have troubles in this fallen world. He also promises that we have victory through our faith because Jesus has overcome the world. If you are facing hard times, be encouraged to push through knowing that you are an overcomer. Read the Word of God to lift your spirits.

"Be strong and courageous. Do not be afraid or terrified because of them, for the Lord your God goes with you; he will never leave you nor forsake you."
Deuteronomy 31:6

Chapter 20
Purpose

Purpose

From the time I was a little girl in elementary school, I've loved to write. When I was eleven years old in the altar, some elderly lady came and told me that I was going to write a book one day on resilience. I didn't even know what resilience was at that time. As I got older into my twenties I said, "I want to write a book on my life." I also said I wanted to be a speaker for women and children that have been victims of abuse. I wanted to show them that there is hope. I used to tell my friend Mieke all the time that I was going to write books and speak one day. Years later in January 2016, I got a Facebook message from Tricia that she was writing a book on resilience and she felt like I was supposed to be in it. I was at a red light in front of the YMCA on the way to church. I will never forget it. I started screaming. I knew that was God. I couldn't wait to get to the church to call Tricia. That's when my journey began. I started right away writing my chapter for the resilience book. As soon as I finished that chapter, I started writing this book on my life. I was looking for a mentor and had put in for one, and it didn't work out, and I was shocked. I was telling Tricia about it, and she said, "I will be your mentor."

That was one of the best things that have ever happened to me. She has impacted my life so much. Let me just say, when God shuts a door, trust him. He will open another one. He knows what's best for his children. That's when my dreams started coming true. I have been coached on speaking and writing, my two favorite things. This is what I have dreamed of for years. Since then, I have coauthored three bestselling books and writing this one. I have also had opportunities to speak. I had been working on this book for two years and writing coauthored books at the same time before the news breaking on Louise's arrest. I have titles for six more books, and I am being led that there will be many more.

God speaks to me all the time about writing. I am definitely in the will of God for my life. I write this chapter to tell you that God created us. He made us. All of the unique things about us such as our gifts, personalities, talents, and so forth are all part of the creation. If you have a dream and it lines up with the Word of God, then it's God. Don't question it. If you step out in faith, God will step in and make the way. We all have a purpose. God knows that purpose before we were ever placed in our mothers' womb. I was told that I was a mistake. That bothered me for years.

I'm here to tell you that no one is a mistake in God's eyes no matter what your parents think. God put us all here with a purpose. You may be nothing to man, but to God you're everything. God knows us inside out. We are to be the hands and feet of Christ, so let him work through you with the desires of your heart that he gave you. One thing I have learned is that sometimes you need to look back at your past. The reason the rearview mirror is small is because you only look back when you need to. The windshield is big because you look forward to getting where you are going. Only look in the rearview mirror at your past for your testimony. Look forward all the other times to get where you are going. Keep moving forward. You may have to crawl at first but just make sure you are moving forward. Don't ever be ashamed of your past. Without the test, we wouldn't have a testimony. Without a battle we wouldn't have victory. Without an impossible circumstance, we wouldn't have a miracle. I don't recall where I heard this, but it has always stuck with me. I tell my kids you have no victory without a fight, no healing without a sickness, no promise without a price, and no test without a testimony.

A lot of what we go through helps us with our calling. I tell people all the time, don't feel sorry for me because of my past because my past has made me who I am today. I couldn't do the ministry that I do without my past. I wouldn't have the compassion I have without my past. I'm one of the most nonjudgmental people you will ever meet because of my past. My past has made me who I am today. I am today living in my purpose making a difference in the lives of others. I am writing books and speaking to give hope. I'm telling people all over the world how to break the chains, to be an overcomer, help them find their voice, and tell them that their past does not define their future. So, I challenge you to step out in faith and do your calling. Go make a difference. Live your dream. Dreams do come true.

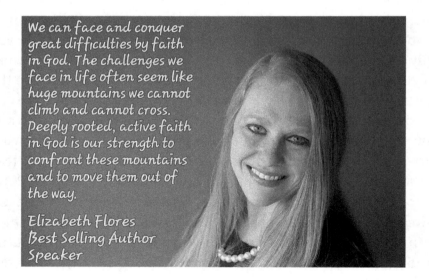

We can face and conquer great difficulties by faith in God. The challenges we face in life often seem like huge mountains we cannot climb and cannot cross. Deeply rooted, active faith in God is our strength to confront these mountains and to move them out of the way.

Elizabeth Flores
Best Selling Author
Speaker

Don't let fear get in your way! Press on! Don't sit there and allow fear to keep whispering in your ear. Get up and move and fight through that lie! Fear is a liar!

Elizabeth Flores
Best Selling Author
Speaker

Your past does not define your future. Everyday is a new day. Keep believing and moving because God has a new plan for your future. Dream and dream big!

Elizabeth Flores
Best Selling Author
Speaker

Chapter 21
Breathe

Breathe

I wrote this chapter before the arrest of my sister Louise. I want to keep it in its original form, so you gain insight to my heart and how devastated I was at the news I received in January of 2018....

I have had many times throughout my life that I felt the walls were caving in on me and I felt almost like I couldn't breathe. Are you feeling this way? Do you feel like the entire world is against you? Do you feel like the walls are caving in on you? Do you feel like you can't breathe? If this sounds like you, I wrote this chapter for you! After sharing so much of my life, I want to share the positive part of it all. My past has made me who I am today. I am an overcomer. I am strong. Most of all, I can minister to other beautiful women and children that are hurting. Because of my past, I am not quick to judge. You never know until you have walked in that person's shoes. I have compassion for people. I see the positive in everything instead of the negative.

If you are the one I'm talking to, I just want to share with you a little. A child being abused can be so traumatizing that they become afraid of their own shadow. I was. A lot of times people think that child abuse only happens to children that are living in poverty. That's not true. It happens in all types of families. Abuse happens all over. It's sad. Types of child abuse include physical abuse, emotional abuse, sexual abuse, and neglect. Children that are abused often suffer physical injuries, emotional scars, malnutrition, and sadly, even death. Child abuse also turns the children from God. These children may struggle to accept God as their loving heavenly Father. Matthew 18:5-6 says, *"And whoever welcomes one such child in my name welcomes me. If anyone causes one of these little ones–those who believe in me–to stumble, it would be better for them to have a large millstone hung around their neck and to be drowned in the depths of the sea."*

As I've been stressing in this book, there is hope. The cycle of abuse can be broken, especially as we give our wounds to Jesus. Most of the time parents who abuse their children have been victims of abuse themselves. Driven by years of hatred and unforgiveness, these parents continue the cycle. That's what I think happened to my sister, Louise, years of hatred and unforgiveness. Parents can lose control by being frustrated by a child's actions or overwhelmed by their own failure or frustration. It can tear a family apart. The Bible gives advice. *"Start children off on the way they should go, and even when they are old they will not turn from it."* (Proverbs 22:6) *"Folly is bound up in the heart of a child, but the rod of discipline will drive it far away."* (Prov. 22:15) Some people view these Scriptures as giving absolute control over their children. This is not true. God's Word should never be used as permission to abuse.

Parents need to discipline their children, but they must discipline, not abuse. There is a big difference. *"Fathers, do not exasperate your children; instead, bring them up in the training and instruction of the Lord."* (Ephesians 6:4) *"Fathers, do not embitter your children, or they will become discouraged."* (Col. 3:21) In God's eyes, there is no justification for abuse. If you are trapped in the cycle and sin of child abuse, commit before the Lord to break this destructive pattern. You are not alone. Jesus knows you better than you could ever know yourself. He will help. *"For we do not have a high priest who is unable to empathize with our weaknesses, but we have one who has been tempted in every way, just as we are–yet he did not sin."* (Hebrews 4:15-16)

Ask God to help you to share your struggle with a trusted Christian friend, or with your pastor. You need to acknowledge the problem and admit you have a problem. Get help before it gets out of hand. If you are the child or someone being abused, you need to know that God has not abandoned you. *"You discern my going out and my lying down; you are familiar with all my ways"* (Psalm 139:3) He knows your pain, and he will heal and restore. Don't be ashamed of the abuse. You are not at fault. Pray and seek God for strength to overcome the abuse. I know it's hard, but you need to forgive your abuser. Unforgiveness can be destructive. God will help you forgive. *"Trust in him at all times, you people; pour out your hearts to him, for God is our refuge."* (Psalm 62:8)

If you are a child or someone in abuse, please seek out help before it gets worse. Tell a family member, church member, a school counselor, or authorities. Remember, forgiveness doesn't mean you have to keep going around this person and putting yourself in the same situation. For example, I forgive my grandfather for what he has done, but I don't go around him or have anything to do with him, and I haven't since I've grown. My kids barely know him. I've never allowed my kids to have a relationship with him. If you are a victim of abuse, remember you are not alone.

Your past does not define your future. You can be an overcomer. You have a voice. Turn to Jesus. Set aside some time every day to read the word. Try to make it the same time every day as long as you read and study every day. This feeds your soul and shows you the way of life. Set aside a time to pray every day. It's important to spend time with the Father. If you don't spend time with your spouse, then you're probably going to grow apart. Well, it's the same with God. It's important to know him well. You will learn his voice if you spend time with him. Break the chains for your children and grandchildren.

I will end this chapter sharing what the Bible says about child abuse. *"Children, obey your parents in the Lord, for this is right.*

Honor your father and mother-which is the first commandment with a promise-So that it may go well with you and that you may enjoy long life on the earth. Fathers, do not exasperate your children; instead, bring them up in the training and instruction of the Lord." (Ephesians 6:1-4)

If you want to find your way back to Christ or develop a relationship with him for the first time, let this prayer be a guide.

Dear God, I am a sinner. I ask you to forgive me for my sins. Cleanse me God. I believe you sent your only son who died on the cross and rose again so that I may be forgiven and have eternal life. I ask you to come into my life and be my Lord and Savior. I repent of my sins. I turn from my wicked ways and trust Jesus as my Savior. I confess that I am born again. In Jesus name I pray. Amen.

"If you declare with your mouth, Jesus is Lord, and believe in your heart that God raised him from the dead, you will be saved."
Romans 10:9

"If we confess our sins, he is faithful and just to forgive us our sins and to cleanse us from all unrighteousness."
1 John 1:91

Just know, it is never too late to change the path you are on. You can come through the other side. You can heal and you can be an overcomer.

Photo Album

Sisters of Secrets

12-25-77

12-25-77

1-7-78

ELIZABETH, LOUISE
TERESA
B-Day St. POW WW 9-16-81

ELIZABETH LOUISE

DEC. 29, 1982

4-11-82

Louise Growing Up

5-24-78

Louise After Marriage

LOUISE ANN ROBINETTE TURP
JULY 1988

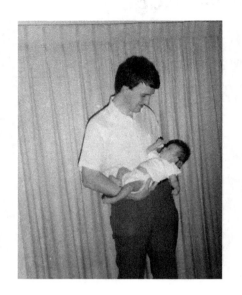

JENNIFER   WAYNE
JOSHUA   JESSICA
                1/2/95

Resource List

Boys Town: 1-800-448-3000
Helping Kids Cope with Unexpected Tragedy

Convenant House: 1-800-999-9999
For teens, kids, and families

National Graduate Student Crisis Line: 1-800-GRAD-HLP or 1-800-472-3457
Helps graduate students reach free, confidential telephone counseling, crisis intervention, suicide prevention, and information and referral services.

National Hopeline Helpline: 1-800-SUICIDE or 1-800-784-2433

National Suicide Prevention Hotline: 1-800-273-TALK or 1-800-273-8255

Postpartum Depression for Moms: 1-800-PPD-MOMS or 1-800-773-6667

Youth Hotline: 1-800-448-1833

Childhelp National Child Abuse Hotline: 1-800-4-A-CHILD or 1-800-422-4453

National Domestic Violence Hotline: 1-800-799-7233

Essential Community Services: 211

It works a lot like 911. The calls are routed by the local telephone company to a local or regional calling center. Types of referrals offered are:

1. Basic Human Needs Resources offers food and clothing banks, shelters, rent assistance, and utility assistance.

2. Physical and Mental Health Resources provides health insurance programs, Medicaid and Medicare, maternal health resources. There are health insurance programs for children, medical information lines, crisis intervention services, support groups, counseling, and drug and alcohol intervention as well as rehabilitation.

3. Work Support offers financial assistance, job training, transportation assistance, and education programs.

4. There are access to services in non-English languages including language translation and interpretation services. These help non-English-speaking people find public resources.

5. Support for Older Americans and Persons with Disabilities includes adult day care, community meals, respite care, home health care, transportation, and homemaker services.

6. Children, Youth and Family Support provides child care, after school programs, educational programs for low-income families, family resource center, summer camps, and recreation programs. It also offers mentoring, tutoring, and protective services.

7. Suicide Prevention gives assistance to suicide prevention help

organizations.

Those who wish to donate time or money to community help organizations can also do so by calling:

National Runaway Safeline: 1-800-RUNAWAY

Drug Abuse Hotline: 1-866-761-6837 or 1-866-948-9865

NOW Mental Health: 1-888-545-8066
Nationwide Facilities for relief from Depression, Anxiety, Eating Disorders. Help with PTSD, OCD, Schizophrenia, and more.

Epilogue

I was ready to publish this book that I have been working on for two years, and the news broke about my sister, Louise Turpin, and her husband going to jail for chaining up their thirteen children while beating and starving them.

At first, I chose to stay quiet. Then I started thinking; since I began my career in writing and speaking two years before this, I had said that I wanted to reach hurting children and women all over the world that have been victims of abuse. So why stay quiet when I can make a difference? I need to get a message to my nieces and nephews along with all the other broken victims all over the world. That message is, "Your past does not define your future. You do not have to be a product of your past. You are not alone." I want to help them find their voice, break the chains in their life, and to be overcomers.

As of this publication I am trying to get a visit with the kids. I will continue to fight to be a part of their lives. I have visited my sister Louise on several occasions and David only once in jail. I attend the court hearings when possible. I am staying involved as much as possible. I continue to search for answers. I am also making my voice heard so that other victims have the courage to speak up. I will, no matter what, continue to stand in love and forgiveness.

I don't know why Louise did these things and we may never know truly what was going through her head. I don't know if maybe she had unforgiveness from her childhood. What I do know is, God will take the bad and turn it around for good if we allow him to. God has used this tragedy to show me that I really need to step up my mission more so than ever.

Abuse is in our families and our backyards. It's time to wake up, reach out, and show the love of God and help these children and women to be overcomers.

Before the news broke I have been working on this book. It has been a book about my life and the abuse that I went through myself.

This is not coincidental. This is God. This book is now dedicated to my thirteen nieces and nephews. It's time for us to rise and be the voices for the abused and to show them the way to overcome and not let their past define their future! It's time to lead them back to God! It's time for us to BE THE HANDS AND FEET OF CHRIST!

About Elizabeth Flores

Elizabeth Flores was born July 31, 1976 and is the second oldest of six children. She was born and raised in Princeton, WV and her family moved to Bristol, TN the last half of her eleventh grade year. She graduated from Tennessee High School in Bristol, TN June of 1995 and then moved to Cleveland, TN to attend Lee University and she traveled with 'Pioneers for Christ' and ministered internationally.

She then met her husband, Jonathan Flores, and got married October 13, 1997. They have seven children Jonathan Jr., Joseph, Jacob, Nicole, Elisha, Ariel, and William (Will). She loves being a mom.

Elizabeth has been through many challenges in her life from child abuse, loss of a baby, and even surviving Cancer. She has always dreamed of writing books and being a speaker to minister to others to share how she overcame her life original 'blueprint'.

She has now started to live her dream and has co-authored three books and has five of her own books that she is currently working on. She is also a speaker. Her message of hope, perseverance, and resilience is one that resonates with people from all walks of life. "I am very excited about my future and the people that will continue to come across my path," she says. "If I can provide teaching and tools to help one overcome hardships like I have experienced, then God is turning my story into a victory!" She and her family live in Cleveland, TN where she is very active in her church.

CPSIA information can be obtained
at www.ICGtesting.com
Printed in the USA
LVHW050838200122
708837LV00011B/643

9 781946 265173